ON THE WAY TO FAITH

ON THE WAY TO FAITH

Personal Encounters with Jesus in John's Gospel

Ken R. Manley

MORLING PRESS
2013

Morling Press
First Published 2013
120 Herring Rd Macquarie Park NSW 2113 Australia
Phone: +61 2 9878 0201
Email: enquiries@morling.edu.au
www.morlingcollege.com

© **Morling Press 2013**

This publication is copyright. Other than for the purposes of study and subject to the conditions of the Copyright Act, no part of it in any form or by any means (electronic, mechanical, micro-copying, photocopying or otherwise) may be reproduced, stored in a retrieval system or transmitted without the permission of the publisher.

The Scripture quotations contained herein are from the New Revised Standard Version Bible, copyright, 1989, by the Division of Christian Education of the National Council of the Churches of Christ in the U.S.A. Used by permission. All rights reserved.

ISBN: 978-0-9922755-1-8

Designed by **Brugel Images & Design** www.brugel.com.au

CONTENTS

Commendations vii

Preface xi

Introduction 1

Chapter 1
'Will you come and follow me?': Jesus and some new friends (John 1:35–51) 4

Chapter 2
'Do whatever he tells you!': Jesus and his mother (John 2:1–12) 12

Chapter 3
'How is it possible?': Jesus and a religious leader (John 2:23–3:21) 21

Chapter 4
'Everything I have ever done!': Jesus and an unhappy woman (John 4:3–42) 30

Chapter 5
'Who can throw a stone?': Jesus and a condemned woman (John 7:53–8:11) 38

Chapter 6
'One thing I do know!': Jesus and a blind man (John 9:1–41) 46

Chapter 7
'If only you had been here!': Jesus and a grieving family (John 11:1–46) 55

Chapter 8
'Smell the waste!': Jesus and a woman who loves him (John 12:1–8) 62

Chapter 9
'Do what I have done!': Jesus and confused friends (John 13:1–20) 71

Chapter 10
'So you are a king?': Jesus and a governor (John 18:28–40) 79

Chapter 11
'What do you do when you're not sure?': Jesus and a doubter (John 20:19–31) 88

Chapter 12
'But do you love me?': Jesus and a guilty friend (John 21:1–19) 95

Conclusion 104

Reading guide 106

Endnotes 108

COMMENDATIONS

"This book deserves slow savouring. Ken Manley's immersion into Jesus' encounters in John's Gospel takes us to deep places of mind and spirit. He tells each story by letting the narrative set the pace, raising key issues with adroit quotes and thoughtful illustrations which accentuate Christ's continuing challenges. We truly find ourselves in these stories afresh. Yes, preachers can learn much here about the serious task of listening to Scripture and designing effective sermons. But for every reader this offers rich food for our ongoing spiritual journeys."

Michael Quicke, C.W. Koller Professor of Preaching at Northern Seminary, Lombard, Illinois

---

"When Ken Manley led us in a series of studies in John's Gospel, how much we looked forward to next Sunday's adventure, to meet another person who encountered Jesus and to find out what happened. It was an uplifting and challenging series because, especially, we were invited to meet Jesus too."

Ken Lyall, OAM, former Principal of Strathcona Baptist Girls' Grammar School and a member of Kew Baptist Church

---

"In this very readable volume Ken Manley writes about the transformational encounters with Jesus experienced by twelve people as recorded in John's Gospel.

Ken Manley needs no introduction to a generation of church pastors and leaders who benefited from his fine scholarship when he lectured in the Baptist theological colleges of South Australia, New South Wales and Victoria.

Others too have greatly appreciated his writing, especially in the field of church history. His outstanding two-volume account of Australian Baptists, *From Woolloomooloo to Eternity,* has become a must read for all those interested in Baptist church history.

This book will allow the reader to benefit from the experience Ken brings from his extensive ministry in pastoral as well as teaching roles. Through the twelve studies readers are invited to explore the possibility of making their own journey of discovery about who Jesus is and his power to bring about transformation.

As Ken notes at the conclusion of the studies, 'In so far as these modest reflections on the encounters with Jesus point to the witness, transforming power and authority of Scripture, we dare to share the same specific goal as the gospel writer confessed, "These are written so that you may come to believe that Jesus is the Messiah, the Son of God, and that through believing you may have life in his name" (20: 31).'

It is a privilege to recommend this book with the confidence that readers will discover the similarities with their own stories of encounters with Jesus."

Rev. Keith Jobberns, National Ministries Director, Australian Baptist Ministries

---

"The encounters between Jesus and all sorts of people in John's Gospel have long been a source of inspiration, reflection and delight for generations of Bible readers. Ken Manley has done us all a great service by re-visiting these encounters in a wonderfully engaging book of reflective sermons.

Ken writes in the same spirit as the author of the fourth Gospel, inviting us to enter into the dialogue and drama of meeting the mysterious stranger from Galilee.

But be warned! This is not a pious set of sanitised sermonettes staying comfortably within the tram-tracks of predictability. Like the stories themselves, these reflections are liable to turn our expectations up-side-down, startle us with their twists and turns, and challenge us with profound insights, puzzling questions and wry humour.

No matter how long we've been on the way to faith ourselves, or even if we haven't begun, there is much to learn from this series of unexpected encounters between Jesus and his new friends, his mother, a religious leader, an unhappy woman, a condemned woman, a blind man, a grieving family, a woman who loves, a confused friend, a governor, a doubter, and a guilty friend.

The open and engaging questions at the end of each chapter make this an ideal guide for personal or group study, especially as Ken draws frequent analogies with contemporary issues, books and films.

I heartily recommend *On the Way to Faith* as a wonderful resource for the church today!"

Dr Keith Dyer, Professor of New Testament, Whitley College, MCD University of Divinity, Melbourne

---

"At its heart, *On the Way to Faith* is a book about encountering Jesus through Scripture and so this is a sorely needed resource for leaders today. As readers are taken through John's account of encounters that people had with Jesus, they are faced with the question, 'Where am I on my journey towards faith in Jesus Christ?' This is a book which has good exegesis, imagination and relevance for the believer and non-believer. Ken Manley brings out contemporary issues such as greed, hypocrisy, doubt and caring for the marginalised as the characters in John's Gospel struggle to come to faith in Jesus. It is a wonderful tool for private devotions as well as for preaching use, with the aim that those who hear might come to know and believe in the one who calls them to follow him."

Rev. Karina Kreminski, Senior Pastor at Community Life Church Cherrybrook

"This is a lucid and well researched discussion of twelve personal encounters with Jesus. Ken Manley's engaging treatment of selected passages from John's Gospel will enrich the spiritual life of anyone who chooses to read it. Suitable for personal study and Bible study groups, it reflects the pastoral heart, scholarship and mature considerations of this highly respected church leader."

Dr Peter Stiles, Adjunct Professor of English and Religious Studies, Trinity Western University, Canada

---

"Ken Manley's sermons, inspired by John's Gospel, are unapologetically Christological and remind us of the Jesus who offers us not just something to believe in, but someone who will transform us. In an era in which the place and power of the sermon are constantly questioned, this collection is a compelling example of the ways in which a gifted teacher with carefully chosen words can uncover the many layers of an ancient story to reveal wisdom which transcends time and place. Ken Manley's book is both a gospel lesson and a class in the craft of preaching."

Rev. Carolyn Francis, Associate Minister, Collins Street Baptist Church

PREFACE

I guess well into my seventies I should be old enough to know better. Who reads books of sermons these days? Who even listens to sermons? Why should I imagine anyone would really be interested in this series preached to a thoughtful congregation at Kew in suburban Melbourne a couple of years ago?

Yes, this is a book of sermons. I have not attempted to 'doctor' them to read like a theological treatise. They are sermons, substantially as they were preached. So, why?

For one thing, a number of listeners asked me to do this. Over the years I have gladly shared notes or even published a few sermons in one place or another. I hesitated about these Kew sermons, however, knowing how often this group of kind and generous people encourages preachers — no matter how well they have really done! I have benefited from such patient listeners since I was a teenager in western Sydney. I recall with a mixture of embarrassment and gratitude many such kind people. My friends at Kew have persisted on this occasion and they must share the blame for this book.

I know that reading a sermon is never the same as hearing a sermon. Preaching is essentially an oral and an aural experience. As John Claypool insisted, preaching is an event, 'something that happens so wholistically that it leaves the kind of impact on one that accompanies participation in any sort of decisive happening'.[1] Even hearing a sermon online or on a CD or DVD, whilst helpful and possibly better than reading a sermon, is not the same. The context of a live worshipping community hopefully transforms the sermon from just another speech into a decisive encounter with God and his people.

There is a fundamental mystery in preaching and declaring 'the Word of God'. Martin Luther once remarked, 'People generally think: "If I had an opportunity to hear God speak in person, I would run my feet bloody… [but] I see only a pastor"'.[2] Yet through the stumbling words of pastors, God has chosen to convey his living Word.

I also know that across many years reading the sermons of others, some by famous preachers of various theological persuasions, has helped me. In this way I have learned much about preaching and have been challenged to be a better communicator of God's Word. I hope that something of that might happen for readers of these sermons.

There is another reason, the main reason in fact, that prompts me to offer this particular series of sermons. Ever since, as a young theological student, I read Emil Brunner's classic theological text *The Divine–Human Encounter* I have been fascinated by the concept of a faith encounter, of a spiritual journey.[3] I also recall reading years ago a fine book of sermons by London preacher Dr A. L. Griffith, *The Crucial Encounter: The Personal Ministry of Jesus* where this idea was developed.[4] The power of the image has perhaps been marred by overuse but as I have tried again to read John's Gospel, the repeated call to a personal encounter with the living Jesus still challenges me to my core.

That is my hope for this book. I have spent most of my adult life as a teacher and pastor and I still thrill to share the divine invitation that comes from Jesus through his Word.

These stories have fascinated artists and poets across the ages and I am grateful to Sheree Brugel of Morling for her selection of classical paintings to illustrate each chapter.

I express my sincere thanks to all at Morling Press for their support. It is a pleasure to be associated again in this way with the College where I was a student and a member of the faculty for several years. I am proud to be one of George Morling's 'men' as I was a student there in his last three years (1958–60) as Principal. I would like to think that the kind of expository preaching which he both encouraged and exemplified is reflected in these studies.

Barbara Coe has cheerfully helped me with editing and formatting of the text and I am in her debt.

Most preachers welcome feedback and encourage discussion of their sermons. Interested readers may wish to explore these studies in a group and my friend Warren Stone, former Principal of Kilvington Baptist Girls' Grammar, has kindly helped me prepare the questions which are included at the end of each chapter.

It was among Baptists that as a teenager I first heard talk about a 'personal encounter with Jesus'. Although puzzled by this phrase, I eventually found it was a true description of a transforming experience and know it is possible for all who will listen and truly seek Jesus.

This is my prayer for these simple studies: that all who read will meet Jesus in a personal way. We may be at different points on the way to faith but reading the Gospel of John will call us all to a deeper encounter with the One who is the Way, the Truth and the Life, as John so memorably recorded (14:6).

Ken R. Manley

1646-1650, St. John the Evangelist on Patmos, Alonso Cano

INTRODUCTION

In March 2012, after a public and courageous struggle with cancer, former footballer Jimmy Stynes died in Melbourne at the age of 45. A state funeral was held in his honour and thousands gathered to pay tribute to him. His story was remarkable. He came from Ireland as a young man and played Australian Rules football for the Melbourne Football Club. Stynes became a football 'legend' — possibly only those who live in Melbourne can fully appreciate what this means. But his fame as an athlete and as leader of his club is only part of the reason why so many mourned his passing. Jim 'reached out' to many others and established the Reach Foundation for underprivileged youth. Numerous young people found that meeting the unassuming but inspiring Jimmy Stynes helped give their lives new directions. As one young friend lamented after his death, 'He has really shaped who I am today and I'm scared of what life is going to be like without Jim here'.[1]

These studies are an invitation to meet a friend who can shape our lives but who will never leave us. I recognise that this is a big leap — from a contemporary figure to one whom we cannot see and know in the same way. The popular apologist for atheism Richard Dawkins, for example, has mocked those who claim to justify their faith on the basis of a 'religious' vision or experience.[2] Many of us, however, affirm that genuine religious experience is still found, not merely by thinking about God — important though that is — nor after some ecstatic vision, but by simply accepting the witness of Scripture to the God who has come to us in Jesus. As Christopher Marshall has expressed it, faith is 'a mixture of mental conviction and existential commitment'.[3] By this kind of faith, Jesus becomes known as a real person who reshapes and guides our lives.

Even the most casual reader of the Bible notices that the Gospel of John is different from the other three gospels of Matthew, Mark and Luke. It is constructed differently and is designed to help us understand who Jesus is and what his life and death mean for us all. That is why these studies are all drawn from John.

Over and over again, through one dramatic encounter with Jesus after another, John shows how people came to faith in Jesus Christ. John introduces us, for example, to a small group of genuine seekers, a religious leader who secretly comes to Jesus by night, and a 'foreign' woman Jesus meets at a well in the middle of the day. So it goes on. Various kinds of people are appropriate subjects in Jesus' gospel. Inquirers only become disciples through a personal encounter with Jesus for themselves.

As Ben Witherington notes, these people did not manifest a full Christian faith in Jesus as the one who died and rose again for the sins of the world. 'They believed, but were only on the way to becoming full-fledged disciples of Jesus… The faith of these characters in Jesus is seen as salutary, but only the first step along the way to a belief in Jesus as the Word of God.'[4]

How is such an encounter with Jesus possible for us today? Simply, with imagination and an open spirit we need to place ourselves in these stories and let God speak to us. We may be at different points along the way to faith. These stories show how the disciples and others who met him were slow learners and only gradually came to see who Jesus was and learnt what following him really means.

'The evangelists were not intent on providing material for conciliar definitions, nor were Jesus and his disciples theologians giving seminars… they were witnessing to the all-transforming gift of God.'[5] Allow John to tell you the stories, one after the other. He has explicitly told us why he has selected these stories: 'These are written so that you may come to believe that Jesus is the Messiah, the Son of God, and that through believing you may have life in his name' (John 20:31). If we sincerely seek faith then John is a sure guide.

(I am not concerned here to raise critical questions about this gospel such as its date, or the community of faith for whom it was first written or even who wrote it [the text does not specifically tell us]. In brief, I am happy to call the author John, and am not uncomfortable with the traditional view that the gospel originates from the Apostle John, the disciple whom Jesus loved (13:23) and an eyewitness of much that he tells us. A brief list of useful commentaries is included in the reading guide and these not only offer more technical detail but also deal with background questions for those who wish to survey the wide range of modern views about the Gospel of John.)

1516, Saint Philip the Apostle, Albrecht Dürer

Chapter One

'Will you come and follow me?' —
Jesus and some new friends
(John 1:35–51)

I once met Sir Donald Bradman. For years I had known about him — the best batsman ever to play cricket. I knew much about him but I did not know him. So when I was a visitor at the Adelaide Rotary Club in 1969 and my friend Allan Tinsley said, 'Who would you like to meet?' I did not hesitate to nominate 'the Don'. We chatted pleasantly and I have never forgotten the day I met him. Meeting Bradman did not change my life (or my cricket skills!) and I could not of course really claim to know him, although I enjoyed the experience.

A few other people, none of them famous, did however shape my life and knowing them changed me. Most of us can remember, for example, a teacher who inspired us. I recall with special gratitude several ordinary suburban people who introduced me to Jesus in a way that was relevant and life-transforming.

These stories in John's Gospel tell us about how meeting Jesus changed people's lives. We are from different times, different cultures, different lifestyles and face different problems. Yet these stories contain powerful spiritual concepts that can bring new meaning to us today. John records a series of narratives in which a wide variety of people respond to Jesus in one way or another. These encounters can still challenge us. We are questioned about whether we will follow him.

There is a difference between studying Jesus, say, as recorded in the gospels, and actually knowing him in one's life. The reader of these stories is placed in a crisis of decision. As in this first story, a private conversation is gradually enlarged to include us all. We are judged by what we read. John says that the Word became *flesh* and *we* beheld his *glory* (1:14); the clear implication is that not all saw the glory; some saw only the flesh. Again and again in John, people misunderstand Jesus; they see but do not perceive. 'The Word of God upon the ear is a whisper and not all hear it.'[1]

1. A chain of witnesses (1:35–41)

'Witness' is a major motif in John. John the Baptist was a witness (1:6–8), as we are told in that profound opening of the gospel. This 'witness' (stressed again in 1:19) points to Christ as the Lamb of God who takes away the sin of the world (1:29). John the Baptist, in many ways a rather scary figure, attracted followers or disciples, people who believed his witness and were seekers after God.

Our story begins with two of these followers leaving John the Baptist and going after Jesus. As William Temple put it: they are 'the first in the long roll of followers. And they follow, as do most of us, because of what they have heard another say.'[2] This line of witness runs back to Christ and those about him. Perhaps it wasn't easy to move on from John but a radical decision is an important quality of true discipleship. There can be no compromise; indeed, to truly understand John the Baptist's role is to follow Jesus. Let us be clear — to follow Jesus means we are to abandon our prior faith commitments.

So, they follow Jesus who then turns towards them. Almost the first recorded action of the Word upon earth is that he turns to seekers — meeting them halfway, as it were, as God always does with genuine seekers. And this Jesus, as we who have read the prologue know, is the Word of God become flesh. He takes the initiative. What are the first words of the Word? A question. 'What are you looking for?' or, 'What do you want?' Literally, 'What are you seeking?' God always takes the initiative and precedes our search.

This is a searching question. He invites them to remain open to what is to be revealed. As McHugh comments, with matchless lucidity Jesus addresses 'the primordial existential question of the world'.[3] The question is itself, almost by nature, a kind of grace, suggests F. D. Bruner.[4] How can we know what we really seek until we have found it? We have a sense of absence, a longing for understanding and meaning. God has made us with this longing.

How do we react to this question of Jesus, 'What do you really want in life?' Many reasonable answers might be offered — a successful career, a happy family life, and a life of peace and purpose — but Jesus presses these potential followers to be open to what he can offer. Are we open to the same possibility?

Their answer at first seems odd. 'Rabbi (a term of respect for a teacher, as John tells us) where do you live?' (1:38).What they were asking evidently was not so they could add his name to their ancient equivalent of an address book, but rather a polite hint that they would like to talk with him at depth. The word 'live' or 'stay' is the word we know in older translations as 'abide' — 'abide in me' (15:4). So they were perhaps seeking something that remains, that stays — in John we constantly encounter layers of meaning in even the simplest of words.

Jesus replies, 'Come and see!' The invitation is not to come to some Bedouin's tent or roadside inn. Readers of the gospel will soon learn that Jesus 'stays' with the Father. They are asked to move to a new level of understanding — to 'see' in John is always to enter into the mystery of God's revelation in Jesus. So they went and they stayed with Jesus.

The importance of being a witness is then illustrated by what Andrew does (1:40–42). He becomes the first missionary. We do not know a great deal about him but he was always bringing people to Jesus. He brings the lad with the bread and fish to Jesus (6:8) and he brings the Greeks to Jesus (12:22). But we know a great deal about his brother — and Andrew led Peter to Christ. 'Perhaps it is as great a service to the church as ever any man did', suggests William Temple.[5] Andrew did not know it all, but shared what he had already experienced.

Have we forgotten that the most fundamental and effective Christian testimony is the private witness of a friend to a friend? This 'friendship evangelism' is not to be reduced to an invasive formula but remains a basic means of sharing faith. We talk today about 'contextual evangelism' which is simply, as in this story, beginning where people are!

2. A new character (1:41–42)

But they were only beginning a journey and their understanding had a long way to go. Andrew says 'We have found the Messiah' (again John tells us what the word means: 'Anointed'). They have not gone beyond their own role in what took place — '*we* have found…'. They have not understood the significance of Jesus' initiative in turning to them, addressing them, and calling them to go further than they intended or expected. They have themselves been sought and found by the Father (4:23). In 15:16, Jesus says to his disciples, 'You didn't choose me. I chose you'.

The divine initiative and authority are revealed by what Jesus says to Simon, 'You will be called Cephas'. 'You are… you will be. You are eager, impulsive, generous, loyal and tragically unreliable. But you will be changed into "Rock-man". A new name conveyed a new identity. Something will happen to him, 'You will be called…'.

To be a disciple of Jesus is not only a matter of finding and following, but also of accepting what Jesus has to give. When a person comes in faith, Jesus can make that person strong at the precise point of apparent weakness. That will become even clearer through the gospel.

What Jesus says to Peter strongly suggests that to call him 'Rabbi' and 'Messiah' is true, but not the whole truth about Jesus, as John's Gospel will show. Jewish expectations of the coming Messiah are not what they are to discover about Jesus.

3. A call from Jesus (1:43–44)

John details successive 'days' carefully and most commentators suggest there is a pattern of development unfolded by this device. So 'the next day' Jesus goes to Galilee and meets Philip.

Jesus says, 'Follow me'. Philip is the only one called by name and reminds us of the stories in the other gospels about the calling of the others to leave their fishing nets — presumably at a later stage, after these initial contacts as described in John.

Philip then immediately becomes a witness too. The circle of faith widens. The pattern of witness is clear: they heard, they sought, they experienced, they witnessed. As soon as Philip is called, he goes to Nathanael and says, '*We* have found', although in his case the reader knows that Jesus in fact found him. As soon as he becomes a disciple he also becomes a missionary — that is the only true discipleship. Disciples need other disciples in order to become disciples.

In verse 45, Philip describes Jesus to his friend. He is the one promised in the Old Testament and (incredibly!) he is the son of Joseph from Nazareth! Nazareth!! Can anything good come from Nazareth?(1:46).

Like us, Nathanael tends to evaluate a stranger by his place of origin or residence (or in our cities, what school he went to or what footy team he supports!). His response is an intelligent question, 'How could this possibly be?' Philip's response is simple: join in the inquiry of faith, 'Come and see'. What Jesus had first said to Andrew and Peter, Philip now repeats to Nathanael.

We love to share good news with friends. Come and see our new house! Come and see the new baby! It is important to come and see for yourself. So here, there is no argument, just an invitation by one who has found a miracle, to a friend that he should come and see for himself. This is a vital lesson in witnessing as opposed to browbeating those of other faiths or no faith. Simply, to go and say to your friends and family, 'Come and see. You must come and see for yourself this Jesus of Nazareth. You need to know firsthand his love, his compassion, his kindness, his mercy, and his beauty. It will make all the difference in your world and in your life'.

Chapter One

'Come and see.' Such simple, open and inviting words. Words that sum up not only the heart of the Gospel of John, but the whole Christian life.

The conversation between Jesus and Nathanael is significant. Jesus greets Nathanael (1:47) and there is a word play. He is a descendant of Israel (whose earlier name of Jacob means 'deceitful') and so he is hailed as 'an Israelite in whom there is no guile'.

Nathanael is puzzled. 'How do you know me?' Jesus' reply is that he saw him under the fig tree. This has intrigued interpreters but most suggest that the fig tree was a place of prayer and meditation. To the astonishment of Nathanael, Jesus knows him as an honest if private seeker, and so Nathanael is moved to add to the confessions given to Jesus: Rabbi. Son of God. King of Israel. He hails Jesus as the fulfilment of Jewish messianic hopes. He was, as Jesus said, a true Israelite, a paradigm of believing Israel.

4. 'Something greater' (1:50)

But to believe on the basis of the wonder of Jesus having seen him under the fig tree is not enough (1:50). This is an incipient faith, but in John there is much more to know about Jesus.

Yes, there is much more. And Jesus opens up a vision of faith, of 'greater things' that cannot be seen with human sight. What is important here is to stress that the 'you' in verse 51 is plural; it includes not just Nathanael, but us as readers. The conversation narrative has become a sermon. The vision is of heaven opened, that is, of an open communication between God and humanity. The old story of Jacob's dream in Genesis where the angels of God went up and down the ladder (28:10–12) is now focused on Jesus, for they are ascending and descending on (yet another title) the 'Son of Man'. He has become Jacob's ladder between heaven and earth. The sacred place where heaven and earth are linked is not Bethel (which Jews honoured as the site of Jacob's dream), but Jesus, the Word made flesh. What had been only a dream to Jacob was a fact for Jesus.

Here is an ancient human desire: 'O that you would tear open the heavens and come down!' (Isaiah 64:1). What is more unlikely than heaven touching earth?

Heaven is where love reigns, where there is room for all God's children at the table. Not at all what earth is like. We know what earth is like. A glance through the morning paper shows us a world that couldn't be more different from God's realm of love. And yet, in Jesus, the unexpected happens. And Nathanael sees it. Heaven gets a foothold on this earth. Jim Wallis of Sojourners says, 'In Jesus, God hits the street'. Nathanael will walk that street, too.

Nathanael will see 'greater things' indeed. And so may we. The 'greater things' are for those of us who did not see Jesus alive on earth. As Jesus said to Thomas after the resurrection, 'Blessed are those who have not seen and yet have come to believe'.

The first disciples followed the one who called them. He still calls ordinary people like us.

The disciples' initial following was only a beginning, a 'precursor of real discipleship'. As Jesus told Nathanael, 'You haven't seen anything yet!' (1:50). But they had begun. The question for us is, are we willing to take that first step along the way to faith?

The Iona Community has a lovely song in which the haunting question of Jesus comes across the ages to us still:

> Will you come and follow me,
> if I but call your name?
> Will you go where you don't know
> and never be the same?[6]

Discussion questions

1. What is it about Jesus that people still find so relevant?

2. Read 'A chain of witnesses' (1:35–41)
   Are you aware of seemingly insignificant links in this chain of witness in your own life but who have proven vital in your spiritual journey?

3. Read 'A new character' (1:41–42)
   In what ways might the life of the Christian disciple be termed a 'journey'? Is this helpful?

4. Read 'A call from Jesus' (1:43–44)
   When people heed the suggestion to 'come and see' Jesus, do they share a common reaction to him?

5. Read 'Something greater' (1:50)
   How can it be said, 'In Jesus, the unexpected happens'?

1304-1306, The Wedding at Cana, Giotto di Bondone

Chapter Two

'Do whatever he tells you!' —
Jesus and his mother
(John 2:1–12)

In October 2008 in the town of Marino, south of Rome, a miracle happened. In dozens of homes people turned on their taps and, instead of water, wine started flowing. Every year, during the Grape Festival, as part of the celebrations to recall a famous sixteenth-century battle victory, the central fountains in the town are switched from water to provide wine. But in 2008, as Mayor Adrian Palozzi explained, 'Due to a technical error, we channelled it into some local homes. Some of the people thought it was a kind of present from the council, but it only lasted three minutes and we corrected it'.[1]

The 'miracle' was a mistake and was easily explained. If it was a sign, then what it revealed was 'a technical error' (bureaucrats speak the same language all around the world), that is, the incompetency of the town's plumbers! Many of those things we call miracles are similarly a matter of exaggeration or a mistake. Football supporters will enthuse about a miraculous goal, or some unusual gift comes our way, and we call it a miracle.

But this miracle when Jesus changed water into wine is of a different order. The story is rich in symbolism and introduces many themes of the gospel: 'the hour' of Jesus; water as a symbol of the new life that Jesus brings; the 'glory' of Jesus.

In John, this is the first of several wonders that he calls 'signs' (2:11). But it was a very quiet affair and very few seem to have noticed that it had happened. John's purpose is rather to trace for us how encounters with Jesus produced faith in his followers. The signs reveal the glory of Jesus, but not all see the truth of the signs. This encounter is initially between Jesus and his mother and leads to her expression of faith and to the disciples also believing in him (2:11).

We can work through this story by fixing on nine points.

1. A wedding (2:1–2)

The story begins. We are told when ('after three days'), which gives the story a 'resurrection aura';[2] the occasion (a wedding feast); where (at Cana in Galilee); and at least some of those who are there (the key people for our narrative, the mother of Jesus, Jesus and his disciples).

Today we are fascinated by different national customs associated with a wedding. In those days it was an exciting and extended celebration, even for the poorest families. The mother of Jesus was there (incidentally, Mary is never named in John) so it has been assumed that perhaps this was the wedding of some of her relatives. We are not told one solitary fact about the bride or the groom, though legends have supplied many guesses as to their identities.

It is a sad commentary on how intervening centuries have so often depicted Jesus as a stern 'kill-joy' type of figure, that we need to stress that Jesus was at the wedding, with his disciples, and fully entered into the spirit of the occasion. He could laugh, eat and drink with his family in a natural and wholehearted way.

We also need to recall that marriage was a traditional symbol of the messianic time and the messianic fullness in Israel (see Hosea 2:19–20; Isaiah 25:6–8; and don't forget Song of Songs!).

Jesus and his friends have been invited (2:2) which answers the suggestion (as some propose) that because they had turned up — uninvited — there was a shortage of wine and that was why Mary was so worried about it.

2. A problem (2:3)

They ran out of wine! From a traditional Baptist point of view it might be a little hard to see how running out of wine constitutes a crisis! Rather a good thing? But if we put ourselves in the context of ancient Galilee, we can perhaps understand why this was such a major concern. Wine was a standard part of daily life. As Bruner notes, 'Wine is celebrated in Scripture; drunkenness is deeply deplored and condemned'.[3]

In a wedding, the honour of the groom's family was at stake. If you couldn't put on a suitable wedding feast, you would lose face in the community. A wedding feast, by the way, typically lasted for the better part of a week. To run out of wine was a serious embarrassment; such an embarrassment had grave social consequences.

3. A conversation (2:3–4)

If some of us have a problem with Jesus providing a huge supply of wine, others of us also worry about how Jesus evidently spoke to his mum. Understanding this conversation is important for an appreciation of what is happening in the story.

Mary doesn't actually ask Jesus to do anything but simply tells him what the situation is. 'They have no wine.' But then Jesus replies, well, what does he say in 2:4? Some translations try to protect us a little by having Jesus call Mary, 'Mother'. In the original, and in most translations, it is simply, 'Woman'. That sounds a little harsh and distant although in Greek it is not necessarily so; recall that on the cross Jesus with great tenderness said to Mary, 'Woman, here is your son', referring to the 'disciple whom Jesus loved' (19:26). But to translate it as 'lady' or 'madam' is too formal.

But what Jesus then said is even more problematic. Translators worry about how to render it. Literally it reads, 'What to me and to you?', a Hebrew idiomatic phrase that is hard to interpret. Is it a statement or a question? John is 'a master of irony and an artist in double meanings'.[4] No matter how hard we try, I think we cannot avoid the impression that some form of rebuke is conveyed. He is saying — at the least — 'What has that to do with me?'

Even more significant is what Jesus then says, 'My time (literally, 'hour') has not yet come'. There is a tension that we cannot miss. Jesus is no longer simply a member of the Nazareth family; the family of faith is what matters. Mary stands outside this mysterious 'hour' that is to become so important in John. The 'hour', readers will discover, will be his violent death, but in John that is also the moment of his glorification through which he will return to the Father who sent him. His ministry at Cana begins the move towards the eventual chiming of his 'hour'. There is a strong sense that there is a 'not yet' in his public ministry as he prepares for his 'hour' (see 7:6, 30; 8:20; 12:27).

Jesus is then clarifying — even to his loved mother — that his most basic response will be to someone else — to his Father — and not to her.

4. A command (2:5)

Mary displays a deep trust in her son: 'Do whatever Jesus tells you to do'. This is not apathetic resignation, a shrugging of the shoulders — the 'whatever' so loved of teenagers today — but an expectant faith. What Jesus does flows from his oneness with the Father, but her command to the stewards depends entirely on her unconditional trust in the power of his word. She believes that the word of Jesus is all-powerful. Her faith is the catalyst for what Jesus does and she is the first to show the quality of true belief in Jesus. As Witherington suggests, 'She too is depicted as a person on the road to full comprehension and full discipleship'.[5]

This saying is a watchword for disciples of all ages: 'Do whatever he tells you'. This for John is the essence of discipleship: if we love him we will obey him (15:14). We, who have the whole of this gospel before us, and indeed the whole revelation of the Bible, can have little doubt about what this Jesus asks us to do — the question is whether we will do whatever he tells us. No matter how unlikely or even absurd it may seem to us, as these unnamed stewards demonstrate, they did precisely what they were told — and the miracle happened!

5. A miracle (2:6–8)

The story is told simply but with the necessary details for us to understand. There were no less than six stone water jars containing the water that was used for ceremonial washings as a part of Jewish purification. Stone jars were useful because they did not become 'unclean'. Six may have symbolic meaning, in that seven is the perfect number and six suggests incompleteness. We may have a clue, some therefore think, to the notion that the Jewish laws and rituals are to be transformed by the power of Jesus. They are large jars, each holding about 100 litres! More than enough for dozens of parties! Such is the extravagance of a God who takes what is good — water — and transforms it into something even more marvellous.

Jesus tells them what to do and, as Mary has asked, they do it. They are then told to take some of this 'water' and give it to the head steward. It is all so simple and there is no fuss. Jesus doesn't stand there and wave his hands about or even see or touch the water! We cannot help but speculate what these servants thought as they went about the task. Were they trying to conceal a grin as they took it to their boss? Or were they aware that something extraordinary was going on right under their noses as they went about a job they had so often done?

Poets have tried to capture the significance. 'Describe the miracle at Cana', the teacher asked her third grade pupils in a class contest. The children expressed how they understood it. The young Lord Byron, later famed romantic poet, wrote, so the story goes, 'Modest water saw its Creator and blushed'. He won the prize.

6. A puzzle (2:9–10)

There is a measure of suspense and humour as the story unfolds. The organiser didn't know where this wine had come from and tells the bridegroom that this is the best wine and he had kept it till last! This went against popular custom, which even the most fervent total abstainer can easily understand — give them the good stuff and when they are past knowing what is going on, give them the poor stuff. (Even, as some cynics have suggested in a vain attempt to explain away the miraculous, give them water and they won't know the difference!)

What the bridegroom made of all this is not recorded but he was presumably somewhat distracted by other events on that memorable day. Nothing is said of the effect this might have had on any of those who were there.

The reader of the gospel will also note the puzzled question, 'Where has this come from?' The ordinary servants know, but their leader does not. The origins of the gift, like the origins of the giver, remain hidden from him. The question of the origins of Jesus recurs in John; in Chapter Four we will see the Samaritan woman confused over the origins of the living water promised by Jesus.

7. A sign (2:11)

What John calls a 'sign' is the clue to the meaning of the event. Of what is it a 'sign'? John tells us clearly, it is the first time Jesus manifests his glory (as in the other gospels this happens on the Mount of Transfiguration). Most see the transformation of the water into wine as being the first act of the living Word in the world, a type of the greater transformation to come. A new age has come! The sign points to something greater. It is not simply a wondrous event; indeed hardly anyone seems to have known it has happened for there is no gasp of wonder or bewilderment as to the power in their midst as is often recorded in other miracle stories. This was the beginning, the first act of the Word in the world.

The signs are not intended to lead us to believe in the power and possibilities of miracles as such, but to lead us to have faith in Christ.

8. A commitment (2:11)

The disciples, who in the opening chapter of John's Gospel stumbled towards Jesus and saw him in terms of their Jewish expectations, now see his 'glory' and believe in him. As John has told us already in 1:14, 'We saw his true glory, the glory of the only Son of the Father'. As Bruner comments, trusting in Jesus is 'a living, repeated, daily movement like breathing or walking'. This is the beginning of that seeing, of true faith. Mary's faith had led others to believe — that, in John, is authentic faith. A new family of faith is brought into being by faith.

And where did all this happen? In a somewhat incredulous tone, John says, his first sign was in the insignificant village of Cana of Galilee. Where is Cana? To tell the truth, we aren't really sure! We think that it was near Nazareth, where Jesus grew up. We don't really know.

You would think that we would know. It gave the world its first glimpse of Jesus' glory. Christian scholars have tried to find Cana but nobody knows for sure.

And that's the point! Jesus could have chosen to start his ministry any place —Jerusalem, Rome — but he chose to start in a small town in the middle of nowhere. You might call it 'ministry at the margins'. So it is interesting that Jesus chose a nowhere place like Cana to start his ministry — ministry at the margins, ministry among ordinary people in an ordinary place.

9. A secret (2:12)

So what follows? They travel on to Capernaum and rest there. No crowds, no feverish public agitation about the miracle. Clearly, very few could have known what had happened. So they rest and travel on, aware that the 'hour' of Jesus lies ahead. It's as though what he did was to be kept a secret. To believe in Jesus is to live a life within a life. Nothing is changed, but everything is changed. What had been water is wine.

Jesus turned water into wine that day in Cana — ordinary water into the choicest of wine — and he's been doing the same thing ever since. Kathy Coffey has written a poem about the couple who were married that day in Cana. She imagines them looking back many years later on the events of their wedding. They say, 'Ever since, it has been miracle'. And by that they don't mean that they have lived anything but completely ordinary lives. But in the midst of those ordinary lives, they have been touched by God. They put it this way:

> Our union was not singular; we fought
> And sulked, sickened like the other folk.
> But in every glass of common water,
> We tasted hints of garnet-gold.[7]

What does it mean that Jesus turned water into wine? It means that life on earth is touched by God. It means that even things that are good are now turned into something better. It means that daily life can be abundant life, because God has broken through the barrier that separates us from him, and has come to be with us, wherever we are.

Perhaps we wish we could have been there to see his glory, to see the worry on the faces of the hosts — and to see worry replaced by amazement — and amazement replaced by joy! But I must admit that I have seen Jesus at work. I have seen him do even more wonderful things than turning water into wine. Many of us can offer the witness, 'Jesus transformed my life! In my life, Jesus has turned water into wine!'

That can happen to any one of us as we do what Mary advised those servants, 'Do whatever he tells you!' **Then we will see his glory everywhere!**

Discussion questions

1. Discuss the ways in which John's use of 'sign' differs from the more common way of calling this a 'miracle'.

2. Read sections 1 to 3 (2:1–4)
   It has been said of some, 'They are so heavenly minded that they are of no earthly use'. In this story, how does Jesus model 'being in the world, but not of the world'?

3. Read sections 4 and 5 (2:5–8)
   Imagine yourself as Jesus' mother, as one of the disciples, and as a steward. What might you have thought before and after the pouring of the water? In what ways might they have thought differently? Why?

4. Read section 6 (2:9–10).
   John is silent about many potentially interesting details of this wedding. What is the effect of this?

5. Read sections 7 and 8 (2:11).
   '… a story that is short, but one with many levels.' What might we glean from the various elements of the story about some of the ways God chooses to work?

6. Read section 9 (2:12).
   Discuss the poem extract by Kathy Coffey. What did Jesus' mother, brothers and disciples take with them into the sober, matter-of-fact, workaday world of Capernaum?

1880, Visit of Nicodemus to Christ, John La Farge

Chapter Three

'How is it possible?' —
Jesus and a religious leader
(John 2:23–3:21)

This is one of the most loved chapters in the Bible. We all know verses like John 3:7 ('You must be born again' NIV) and 3:16 which begins, 'For God so loved the world…'. These create special dangers as well as opportunities for us. The passage is clear, comprehensive and powerful but we are so familiar with it that we may just miss its meaning when we look again at it. For example, how is it possible for a person to be 'born again' and what does that really mean?

The exact phrase ('born again') is only used twice in the whole Bible (both in this chapter), although the idea of regeneration is in many places. Why has 'born again' become such a popular description of being a genuine Christian? Simply, because the hope it embodies still has relevance and hope for all ages.

The American Christian rock band 'Third Day' captures this appeal in their song, *Born Again*, first performed in 2012.

> Well, today I found myself
> After searching all these years,
> And the man that I saw,
> He wasn't at all who I thought he'd be,
> I was lost when You found me here
> And I was broken beyond repair.
> Then You came along
> And You sang Your song over me.
> It feels like I'm born again,
> It feels like I'm living,
> For the very first time,
> For the very first time in my life.[1]

The absolute demand of Jesus, 'You must be born again', reminds us that at the heart of encountering Jesus is a seemingly impossible inner experience, being 'born again'.

Our hope is to discover through these stories in John how Jesus met various people and led them to grow in their faith, and then for us to discover how we too may find that faith, to be born again.

Nicodemus was someone who saw that God was at work in the life and works of Jesus but who struggled to grasp the implications of all that was happening. He was perhaps one of those who had been impressed with the 'signs' that Jesus had performed (2:23). Nicodemus is another model of a journey to discipleship. He approached Jesus from within his own world and, whilst that was inevitable, he struggled to move beyond his own tradition and culture. Jesus challenged him and tried to draw him away into a whole new paradigm of reality. He is a type of the sympathetic Jewish seeker who was still 'in the dark' about who Jesus is.

This chapter is unusual in its structure. We have an introduction of Nicodemus and his secret visit to Jesus (3:1–2), then a dialogue follows and, as so often in

John, this conversation shows misunderstandings and double meanings that are a means to advance spiritual understanding (3:2–10). Then there is a change, a bridge (3:11–12) when the words of Jesus open up into a discourse (the first of several in John) in which the identity of Jesus and God's mission of salvation through him are clearly taught (3:13–21). Salvation or judgement, it is made clear, inevitably flow from the acceptance or refusal of this revelation. The distinction is as absolute as that between light and darkness.

1. Nicodemus meets Jesus (3:1–2)

Nicodemus is introduced in a few words. As Culpepper observes, he is 'both individual and representative, a foil and a character with conflicting inclinations with which the reader can identify'.[2] He is a Pharisee (that sect among the more rigorous Jews who tried to practise every detail of the law) and a ruler (that is, a member of the Sanhedrin, one of the 70 who ruled much of Jewish life — as much as the Romans would allow).

We are told he came 'by night'. How are we to understand this coming in from the dark? We may guess it was perhaps that he came secretly; after all, John has just told us that Jesus had caused quite a stir in Jerusalem by turning over the money changers' tables in the temple (2:13–22) and Nicodemus would not want to be readily associated with this disturbing Galilean. But I think we should note that the contrast between light and darkness is a major theme of the gospel. By coming in from the black night, he is beginning to move towards the light.

2. The conversation (3:2–10)

Nicodemus begins by making a typical Jewish believer's response (like those first fragile believers in Jesus whom we met in 1: 35ff.). His confession of faith is limited. He calls Jesus 'Rabbi' but he does not ask a question; he makes an observation; his approach is from his own Jewish world. Still today, many admire Jesus as a 'teacher'. Jesus is certainly that, but he must be taken seriously and seen as more than that.

The self-confidence of Nicodemus's tradition and culture appear in his affirmation, 'We know…'. Out of his own experience he recognises Jesus as a prophet and a teacher from God; the 'signs' confirm this.

But he falls short of an authentic act of faith, like many others (2:23). He is really only wanting Jesus to confirm what he has already worked out for himself.

Jesus is not overwhelmed or unduly impressed that such a distinguished visitor should seek him out. He answers a question Nicodemus has not asked, 'No one can see the kingdom of God without being born from above' (3:3). Jesus wants to draw him beyond his own expectations.

The double meaning of the words, 'born from above' or 'born again', seems to be lost on Nicodemus, though as readers we are ready for this type of dialogue. Either is a possible translation. Both may be meant: unless a person is 'reborn from above'. But this removes the ambiguity of the phrase in the original. Nicodemus chooses to take the more literal and seemingly impossible meaning. Perhaps he is more wistful than obtuse. Here he is, a relatively mature man; what he is today, he is because of all his yesterdays, and he is as wise as life and learning can make him. Is he being asked to become so infantilised as to forget all his wisdom and traditions and become as helpless and as ignorant as a newborn child?

But Jesus is insistent. You cannot see God's kingdom and you similarly cannot enter into that realm unless you are born 'from above' or 'again'. This is expanded by Jesus in 3:6–8 (and compare 1:12–13). This new birth is 'a matter of transformation, not just more information; new being, not merely new seeing'.[3]

'By water and the Spirit' is variously understood. Some link it with human birth and 'by water' means either the conception (in some Jewish writings 'water' is used for semen) or the birth process. If so, you are born human and then need to be born of the Spirit (3:6). Others want to link it with Christian baptism, but I think we should rather link it with the baptism of John the Baptist who said, 'I baptised you with water but he will baptise you with the Holy Spirit' (1:31 and 33). After all, the movement associated with John had been the most dramatic revival movement in contemporary Jewish life. John's baptism was a symbol of repentance and so Jesus is saying that the new birth requires both repentance and the power of the Holy Spirit. Of course, it should also be noted that students of the Hebrew Scriptures knew that the promised coming of the Spirit was like clean water being sprinkled on a dirty figure (Ezekiel 36:25–27).

Yet what Jesus teaches here is not a 'natural' development out of Israel's history. It is a new birth. Jewish religion, such as seen in Nicodemus, cannot simply move forward into this new kingdom: 'A moment of discontinuity, comparable with physical birth, is essential'.[4]

The contrast is certainly between flesh (or what is human) and the spirit. To be 'born of the flesh' (3:6) means to be happy with what one can control oneself. 'Born of the Spirit' means a different way of seeing and understanding. 'There is no evolution from flesh to spirit' (Hoskyns); a radical rebirth is needed. As Luther taught, it is not what you must do or not do, but concerns what you must become.[5]

Again, there is a double meaning as the word for 'wind' and 'spirit' is the same (in both Hebrew and Greek). The wind is mysterious and powerful; so it is with the Spirit.

Nicodemus cries out in puzzled astonishment, 'How can these things be?' (3:9). But did not Nicodemus know his Bible which spoke about a new creation? Did he not believe in God who could do a new thing? How distant the two men are in understanding one another! They are talking past each other. Jesus rebuked Nicodemus. As Frederick Buechner paraphrases his response:

> Maybe Nicodemus had six honorary doctorates and half a column in *Who's Who*, Jesus said, but if he couldn't see something as plain as the nose on his face, he'd better go back to kindergarten.

> 'I'm telling you like it is', Jesus said. 'I'm telling you what I've seen. I'm telling you there are people on Medicare walking around with the love-light in their eyes. I'm telling you there are [former atheists] teaching Sunday School. I'm telling you there are undertakers scared silly we'll put them out of business… I'm telling you God's got such a thing for this loused-up planet that he's sent me down, so if you don't believe your own eyes, then maybe you'll believe mine… maybe you won't come sneaking around… in the dark any more, but will come to, come clean, come to *life*.'[6]

Perhaps many today can identify with Nicodemus. We have our own understandings. We can only understand what is reasonable. There are today constant tensions in public debates between the 'new atheism' and Christians. What science can demonstrate is to be trusted, but nothing else. As F. D. Bruner suggests, 'Nicodemus is a classic type of the rationalist — only what is humanly reasonable can be true'.[7]

Many admire Jesus ('a good teacher') and in no way would they oppose him or the church; they want to know something of Christ, but in their own way and on their own terms.

But Jesus hits us with this unambiguous assertion. You must be born again. In this postmodern age we don't want talk like that. Jesus cuts through all distinctions — gender, race, education and age — and says that you, all of you, must be born again. (The 'you' in verse 7 is plural, so John is moving beyond the story to a sermon.)

3. The discourse: what the coming of Jesus means for all of us (3:11–21)

The bridge should not be missed. The speaker and the listener are abruptly multiplied. Note how it changes in 3:11 to 'we know'. Jesus is not using the 'majestic plural'; this is an affirmation made by all who believe.

Nicodemus has not been able to grasp the revelation given by Jesus, who stresses that his words do not come from mere hearsay but out of direct contact with God. Will he and Judaism (and we, the readers) ever be able to grasp these heavenly things?

The heavenly origins of Jesus are shown in 3:13–15. Only the Son of Man has come down from heaven (and readers think of 1:18). How will God be shown in Jesus? As Moses physically raised up the metal serpent in the wilderness, so that those who had been bitten by snakes and gazed upon it could be restored (Numbers 21), so the elevated Son of Man will bring life to those who believe. 'Lifted up' has a double meaning: both exalted and lifted up on the cross; that, in John's Gospel, is the 'hour' of his glorification.

Then comes what we have numbered as verse 16. F. F. Bruce observes:

> The essence of the saving message is made unmistakably plain in language which people of all races, cultures and times can grasp, and so effectively is it set forth in these words that many more, probably, have found the way of life through them than any other biblical text.[8]

The word 'love' appears for the first time in John. Not just 'God is love' — a precious truth — but love led God to act at a particular time and place. This love is found even and especially in the 'lifting up' of the Son. God 'gave' his Son, God 'sent' his Son (16–17). These verbs make the love of God a historical event. This is precisely how God loves. As Stanley Jones put it, 'At the cross God wrapped his heart in flesh and blood, and let it be nailed to the cross for our redemption'. What is most intimate and vital to the Father — his only Son — is given for the life of all.

Here we move beyond traditional Jewish beliefs. There is no reserve in God. His love is universal. God loves 'the world'. As Augustine wrote, 'God loves each one of us as if the only one'. His all-embracing love is unrestricted and comprehensive in scope, and the gift of the Son leads to an unlimited gift for all of us who believe — 'eternal life' — describing, not so much the length, but the quality of life.

He is received not by moral effort but by simple trust. God is not limited by the self-destructive capacities of human freedom — he reaches out to evildoers that they may not perish. God is not going to keep passing on the evil that so destroys humans — like some counterfeit coin — but will absorb it in the flesh of his only Son, pay the cost himself, and there it will be finished. So the thrust of the discourse is clear and demands a decision; to accept or refuse will determine one's ultimate identity and destiny. Using the language of 'life', 'light' and 'darkness' stresses the importance of the decision. To refuse belief is to bring self-condemnation, to show clearly that we live in the dark and will always live in the dark.

So we cannot be indifferent. The cross is surely the means of our salvation but it is inevitably an agent of discrimination, of crisis, of judgement. To refuse the greatest gift ever offered? There is nothing worse that can be done to one after that great sadness.

It took Nicodemus some time, we think, to come to true faith. He appears twice later in John: in 7:50–52 he defends Jesus before the Jewish authorities and then in 19:38–42 he is with Joseph of Arimathea in caring for the body of Jesus. I like to think, though it is left open in the gospel, that this means Nicodemus had come to see in Jesus the revelation of God in a new and comprehensive way.

So where are we? Are we struggling with moving beyond our comfort zone? Do we still want to stay with Nicodemus on that dark windy night and in our commonsense way murmur, 'How is it possible?' The puzzle can only be solved in one way: by the act of faith.

The awful possibility is that refusal shows we really do prefer the darkness of unbelief, of not knowing God. Condemnation comes only to those who 'have not believed in the name of the only Son of God' (3:18). The tense of the verb makes it clear that 'unbelief is not just one act but a persevering state of mind which rejects the idea of the fatherhood of God as preached uniquely by Jesus'.[9] Paul was later to put it like this: 'The message about the cross is foolishness to those who are perishing' (1 Corinthians 1:18). Until you believe, you cannot know how it is possible! That is the conundrum of true faith. Isn't it about time that you tested all this 'new birth' and 'eternal life' talk that you have heard about for so long?

Only then will you be able to answer the question of Nicodemus, 'How is it possible?' It is possible by faith in Jesus and his death on the cross, and by trusting that God's Spirit will sweep you away from your old ways and traditions and into a new life.

Discussion questions

1. If possible, reflect on the way you yourself 'came to Jesus'. Did it feel like being 'born again'?
   If appropriate, members of the group might share their individual experiences. What did you find you had in common, and how did you differ?

2. Discuss some of the many contrasts revealed here (and why they matter):
   'admire Jesus as a "teacher"' versus 'seen as more than that'
   the new birth as 'more information' and 'new seeing' versus 'transformation' and 'new being'
   - 'baptised you with water' versus 'baptise… with the Holy Spirit'
   - 'what you must do or not do' versus 'what you must become'
   - 'what science can demonstrate is to be trusted' versus '…but nothing else'.

3. Read sections 3 — 5: (3:11–21)
   What is so important about the 'love of God' being 'a historical event'?

4. Discuss in what ways the cross is to be seen as central.
   'The puzzle can only be solved in one way. By the act of faith.'
   - Explain what this 'puzzle' is.
   - What is this 'act of faith'?
   - Discuss in what ways 'the act of faith' is so important.

1500, Christ and the Woman of Samaria, Juan de Flandes

Chapter Four

'Everything I have ever done!' —
Jesus and an unhappy woman
(John 4:3–42)

She must have trudged that mile scores of times. Day after day after weary day. Every day was the same. The sneers of women and the scarcely veiled leers of men were not so likely in the heat of the day at noon. She wasn't a refugee but often felt like one; certainly she was a marginalised person in that insular society. She walked at a time when others sought shade and she walked to this well that, according to tradition, Jacob had dug centuries before as a gift for Joseph. Every day she walked that mile, even though there was a well in her town of Sychar.

But this day was different. Her life was completely revolutionised. It all flowed from an encounter with a tired stranger sitting alone at the well. The Old

Testament has several stories about significant men meeting women at wells: Isaac (Genesis 24), Jacob (Genesis 29) and Moses (Exodus 2). Now Jesus; perhaps that is in mind as John tells this story.

We have been reading John's Gospel and tracing other encounters with Jesus; most recently his meeting with Nicodemus. This woman is his polar opposite. The contrast between the two could not be greater. There is a wide spectrum of believers in Jesus found in John.

Nicodemus represents the pinnacle of religious achievement in Judaism. He is a man — an important man — known by name and reputation. This woman in our story is not dignified with a name but she is known by reputation. She is a Samaritan — a despised foreigner — with a confused and conflicted past that has led to her shame and unwelcomed reputation. But, as D. A. Carson observes, 'both needed Jesus'.[1]

Nicodemus came by night. She comes at high noon. Nicodemus is a Pharisee, the epitome of strict morality. The Samaritan woman is living with a man who is not her husband. Nicodemus says nothing in response to Jesus, but she rushes back to tell her whole village about this stranger who, she declares, told her everything she had ever done!

So in this story, among the most beautifully crafted stories in the whole Bible — featuring the longest conversation that Jesus had with any one person in the gospels — we see how Jesus led this woman to real faith.

Jesus is the model for all mission — as this encounter shows — and the woman's response is also a remarkable story of mission, for this marginalised woman becomes the first woman witness to her own people and the finest evangelist in the whole gospel.

John does not just affirm that 'God so loved the world' in general, in the abstract. He shows the wideness of that love in this encounter with a woman at a well.

Once again, John invites us into an encounter with Jesus as we read this story. As the Samaritan found this man who knew all about her and offered her the gift of 'living water', so Jesus offers us an intimate awareness of who we are and the water that will refresh our parched beings. Similarly, we will be provoked to think about our mission in the world today, especially about how we interact with the marginalised of our society.

1. Jesus in conversation and mission (4:4–26)

We are told that Jesus had to go through Samaria (4:4). That is not so much a geographical note as indicative of a theological necessity. He was sent (4:34). God so loved the world, including Samaria. He must move into the world beyond Israel, just as the early church was specifically told (Acts: 1:8). John makes clear there was an ancient and intense division between Jews and Samaritans; the gulf was both racial and religious. It was as deep a gulf as that between Israelis and Palestinians, between Serbs and Croatians, between Arabs and Jews today.

The disciples have gone to find food. As someone has remarked, Jesus did not multiply loaves for lunch on a daily basis. Jesus is hot, thirsty and alone at the well. He initiates contact. In so doing he defies all conventions, a Jew talking to a Samaritan — and a man talking in public to a woman, and possibly, an immoral woman at that. She was trebly a minority person: woman, Samaritan, sinner. A strict rabbi was forbidden even to speak to his wife, sister or daughter in public. Some were even called 'bruised and bleeding' Pharisees because they shut their eyes when they saw a woman and so walked into walls and houses. (Some today, by way of contrast, are known to walk into walls because they are too busy looking!)

This direct speaking to the marginalised was typical of Jesus. John Claypool declares, 'He took words that for centuries had functioned as nouns — words like male and female, Jew and Gentile, Samaritan, rich, poor, good, bad — and reduced them to the level of adjectives'.[2] Here Jesus is given the label 'Jew' by the Samaritan woman, while at 8:48 the Jews label him a 'Samaritan'. Both of these labels are given to him in a less than friendly manner, to say the least. He is a stranger to both groups. 'He came to what was his own, and his own people did not accept him' (1:11).

How easily we still categorise people or reduce them to stereotypes — ethnics, asylum seekers, refugees, bogans, homeless, gays. We find it far easier to witness to our own type of people rather than risk genuine engagement across ethnic or class divides. We are so often like the disciples who were clearly incredulous when they returned from the town with some food and saw Jesus with this woman. The possibilities of each life are overlooked when we drop people into such labelled boxes.

Jesus established contact by asking for a favour. Whilst this is always a good strategy for beginning mission work, it must be authentic. He was thirsty and genuinely wanted a drink of water. She must have been surprised as her reply, gently mocking in tone, suggests: 'How is it that you, a Jew, ask a drink of me, a woman of Samaria' (4:9). Once again in the ensuing conversation we have, as in so many conversations in this gospel, misunderstandings and double meanings. Jesus draws her into the conversation — he really listens to her.

When Jesus speaks about the gift of 'living water' (4:10) she understands him to mean 'running water' as from a stream or a spring. Jacob gave this well as a gift. She responds, 'Are you greater than Jacob?' Jesus takes the conversation to a deeper level in 4:13; by the water he means eternal life, offered as a gift. Intrigued, she asks that he might give her that water, 'and I won't have to come here again!'

She only understands very little, but Jesus takes her as she is. Gradually he shows her that the barriers that seemed impossible to breach are being broken by a love that knows no boundaries. Step by step he will lead her on. The fact is that we, too, so often understand so little about faith. But we can be confident that God will take us as we are, with our little understanding, and take us further. Isn't that what we have seen in encounter after encounter in John?

Jesus does not scold her for not understanding. But there is something else holding her back. Jesus unerringly points to her moral confusion by asking her to call her husband. She gives a true but inadequate response, 'I have no husband' (4:17). Jesus simply describes her life. Having had five husbands is not necessarily a sin — they could have died or left her — but it does seem at the least indicative of much pain and heartache. And Jesus also accurately describes her present domestic situation: 'The one you have now is not your husband' (4:18).

There is no hint of moral outrage or judgement in his words. He names the brokenness of her life, not to condemn her, but to let her know with whom she is speaking and to startle her into discerning that Jesus is a prophet.

She tries to avoid this issue by raising a familiar theological argument between Jews and Samaritans (4:20), a device still employed by people when a religious conversation becomes too close for comfort. Her statement is along the lines of, 'We think our church is right and you think yours is right'. Any witness for Jesus today will encounter people who want to talk about past historical tragedies such as the Crusades or who will want to recite the latest scandal in the church. At the same time, it is important for those engaged in mission to know about the belief systems and values of those to whom they are speaking.

But Jesus does not allow himself to be distracted into debate. He declares that true worship of God is not determined by where God is worshipped, but by how. God desires to be worshipped truly and in the power of the Spirit.

The reality of God transcends all our divisions of sex and race and tradition and place — the things we fight about. Jesus insists that the little boundaries that we so happily draw up are irrelevant: 'God is spirit and those who worship him must worship in spirit and truth' (4:24). A new era of grace has arrived. God is not confined to the hallowed sanctuaries of either Samaria or Judea but is revealed as the Father to whom all are welcome to come in intimacy and assurance.

When the disciples return with their withering and puzzled looks, she runs off to her village and, as John notes, leaves her water jar behind — she is coming back. She is so excited that she must first tell others.

The disciples now engage in conversation and again there is misunderstanding, this time about food (4:31–33). The misunderstanding, as with the 'water' conversation, leads Jesus to clarify his spiritual meaning. His 'food' is his mission.

2. A witness and a believing response (4:39–42)

Her witness is simple (4:29). She doesn't preach to the villagers, she doesn't try to teach them. She simply points them to Jesus. Her witness is so simple and incomplete. I have seen a man who told me everything. '"He told me all that I ever did" is not exactly a recitation of the Apostles' Creed.'[3] She is not altogether sure about who Jesus is: 'Could he be the Messiah?' But what she does say is simple and powerful: 'Come and see for yourselves!' Once again, as in chapter 1, 'come and see' is the essential invitation of witness (1:39, 46).

Actually, she has herself stumbled towards this belief in Jesus as Messiah (4:25–26). Jesus' reply, 'I am he, the one who is speaking to you', is of course reminiscent of the distinctive name for God in the Old Testament and this gospel will show Jesus saying 'I AM' in a variety of beautiful images.

Whatever her puzzling words, however the townsfolk regarded her, they were all persuaded that something had happened and all rush off to see for themselves. Thank God that her stammering uncertain witness is enough. All it ever takes is an honest and faithful pointing to the one who is truly the wellspring of eternal life. The witnessing word need not wait upon having faith in full measure. As Craddock says, the Word of God is such that it can generate in listeners a faith that exceeds that of the speaker.[4] That's the assurance that every preacher and every witness needs.

What did she mean when she claimed that he had told her all she had ever done? This could not have been literally true. But he told her that he knew about the things which mattered in her life, the defining experiences which had made her who she was and about which she had for so long carried a burden that was destroying her life. A penetrating and blunt word spoke to her need. Her spiritual thirst was caused by her selfish lust or her being the victim of such lust (in a male dominated world she may have been more the victim than the perpetrator). It seemed as though he had told her everything she had ever done. As someone suggested, this woman came for water but went home with the well!

With the rich young ruler, the stumbling block was his riches (Mark 10:17–22). 'All I ever did' in his case was of a different experience (making money) but with the same lonely and sad consequence. But unlike the rich young ruler, this woman knew that Jesus understood and he cared. That was enough for her to see that this 'man' was one sent from God.

So Jesus stayed with them, right there in their Samaritan homes. And the powerful conclusion to our story cannot be missed: 'Once we believed because of your witness'. But now Jesus was the Word that brought them salvation (4:41); they declared, in a phrase used only here in John's Gospel, that he is the 'Saviour of the world' (4:42). Not just of Jews, but also of Samaritans and therefore of the whole world. Truly, God so loved the world. This is how it is — we move from a state of dependence on the witness of another to an assurance of personal experience.

Indeed, the role of the woman is suggested by the metaphor that Jesus uses of the harvest: the sower, the reaper and the gatherer all share in the joy of the achievement (4:36–37).

Have we heard Jesus tell us that he knows all that we have ever done? All that defines who we are, the good and the bad? The shame that could overwhelm me — he knows all about me! But that is only so that we can know his love. He listens to us and offers us cleansing water that can refresh our souls.

In any century, our response to the Lord is the same. He tells us he knows all about us. We confront our true selves, experience God's grace and share the good news. It's that simple! Why not begin by accepting the witness of your friends and of the Christian community — and then as you go on further in your journey you too can come to know Jesus as your Saviour, this Saviour of the world.

Discussion questions

1. 'There is a wide spectrum of believers in Jesus found in John.' Summarise some of the types of believers in John. How wide is the range of 'believers in Jesus' that you have heard about or personally know?

2. Read section 1 (4:4–26).
   - What were the positives of Jesus' conversation?
   - In what other ways does his conversation act as a model for us in mission?
   - Discuss the quotation from Claypool beginning, 'He took words that for centuries had functioned as nouns…'.

3. Read section 2 (4:39–42).

4. 'Jesus understood and he cared.' How critically powerful are these factors in our relationships?
   - What were the ingredients of the Samaritan woman's 'successful' witness? How does that shape our understanding of witness today?
   - How important is the distinction that the believing Samaritans drew between 'her' words and 'the word of Jesus' (4:41–42)? Can this also be applied to our witness today?

1644, Christ and the Woman Taken in Adultery, Rembrandt

Chapter Five

'Who can throw a stone?' —
Jesus and a condemned woman
(John 7:53 – 8:11)

Who can throw a stone? This might at first sound like an invitation for parents to get out with their children and start skimming stones across the surface of a lake. But this passage is about something more challenging that involves all of us, parents or not.

This story of the woman taken in adultery has a long and fascinating history. As most modern translations note, it has appeared in different places in the various New Testament manuscripts (some have it in Luke). All of the stories about Jesus began orally — it was a few decades before they were written down — so it is possible that this story was not recorded until much later.

Augustine in the fourth century advanced the misogynous explanation as to why church leaders were nervous about this story: they feared it might prompt their wives to commit adultery!

So the text 'floated' in the written material about Jesus. Yet there is every reason for us to accept this story as a reliable witness to Jesus of Nazareth and we may look to this story as another example of the transforming encounters that Jesus had with various persons.

1. Jesus teaching in the temple (8:2)

As we have it in John, this event takes place at the end of the Feast of Tabernacles where the teaching of Jesus in the temple has alarmed the Pharisees who are ready to condemn this strange man from Galilee.

We are alerted, then, to the possibility of entrapment. The action takes place within the temple, at the heart of Israel's religious and cultural life. Jesus is speaking of life when he is dramatically interrupted by these merchants of death (8:3–4). That this takes place in this sacred space makes their hypocrisy and failure to show mercy all the more ironic. The scene has fascinated artists, most notably Rembrandt who depicts the distressed and dishevelled woman lying at the feet of Jesus and the accusers pointing their fingers.

2. The trapped woman is used to try to trap Jesus (8:3–6)

What has happened? We are told that she was caught in the act of adultery. She is simply referred to as 'a woman'; an object, no name, no voice, and no identity apart from that of an adulterer.

She is placed 'in the middle' of a noisy ring of angry, hostile and probably prurient men — just as still happens in this barbaric form of killing. These 'odious ecclesiastics' (William Temple) spit out their charge: 'This woman was caught in the very act of committing adultery' (8: 4).

Her danger is very real. Then, as in some places still, women are cheap and there are plenty of stones. That is what happens 'to a woman like this' — she is not thought of as an individual but as a kind of female who deserves death. Her reasons for acting in this way are not raised — was she a victim of violence, for example? No, she is just a label that identifies her punishment.

But it isn't all that clear. Questions occur to us and the story tells us what was happening. The scribes and Pharisees wanted to test Jesus (8:6). The woman was a pawn in a power game of these religious partisans. It was all so hypocritical.

Adultery is 'not a sin one commits in splendid isolation'.[1] Where was the man? If they had been caught in the act, both were guilty; had they somehow lost him on the way to the temple? How were they 'caught in the act'? Had it been 'set up' and, if so, were they not also guilty for not stopping such a sin? Where was the husband? Who were the witnesses required by 'Moses', the traditional designation for this Jewish law to which they refer (see Leviticus 20:10; Deuteronomy 22:21)?

How was it a trap for Jesus? If Jesus agreed to her being stoned to death, he would appear to be as bloodthirsty as these 'righteous' men and no longer 'the friend of sinners'. He would possibly find himself in trouble with the Romans who did not permit Jews to inflict capital punishment. If he protested her execution, he would be opposing Mosaic Law. From their viewpoint, it was not this woman but Jesus who was on trial. They were very pleased with themselves.

Readers of this gospel will know, as 1:17 tells us, 'The law indeed was given through Moses; grace and truth came through Jesus Christ'. How will both grace and truth be shown in this situation?

3. The response of Jesus shows up the hypocrisy of her accusers (8:6–9)

Jesus at first said nothing but bent over and 'started writing on the ground with his finger'. Why? What did he write? Numerous guesses have been made, but the text does not tell us. Certainly it adds suspense to the story but it remains an enigma.

Many note Jeremiah 17:13: 'They will disappear like names written in the dust, because they have abandoned you, the LORD' (*Good News Bible*). The suggestion is that this is a prophetic action in the way of the Old Testament prophets. One scholar has ingeniously proposed that whilst seated Jesus could only have written about twelve Hebrew characters and he has found suitable texts of twelve characters. Yet another suggests that Jesus is following the Roman practice of writing down a verdict before reading it.

Perhaps the gesture of Jesus writing in the sand is simply a statement of disengagement, of indifference and even disappointment with the proceedings, a refusal to buy into useless debate. The word for 'writing' can mean drawing or, if you like, doodling; Jesus waits for the crowd to settle down.

The ecclesiastical bullies keep on questioning Jesus. He sits up and gives the famous reply about the first stone, 'Let anyone among you who is without sin be the first to throw a stone at her' (8:7). The 'first stone' is a direct allusion to a passage such as Deuteronomy 13:9 where the first stone is to be cast by the eyewitness. His direction is at once dramatic and devastating. This is high-risk strategy for the woman. Will some overweening hypocrite pick up a rock and hurl it at her?

But the words of Jesus are brilliant. He manages to recognise the Bible's teaching and at the same time to honour his own unique compassion.[2] How many, like these accusers, have used the Bible in a cruel way?

Jesus again kneels down and writes in the dust. Could he be writing their secret, sexual sins? One manuscript rather improbably suggests he wrote 'the sins of each of them'. Whatever he wrote, the next sound was a gentle thud as the first stone was dropped. The oldest man quietly turned and walked away. Was he most conscious of the responsibility given by the gift of years? Thud after thud, the stones were dropped. One by one the accusers left — eventually the fascinated crowd, having held its collective breath, sighed and also slipped away. As Augustine famously said, 'Only two remain, the wretched woman and the incarnation of mercy'. For the first time, the woman is addressed and has a voice. Jesus does not question her about her alleged sin but asks, 'Where are the accusers'?

She is no longer the object, a 'sex object', but a truly acting human subject. He invites her to interpret what has happened. Her whispered reply is brief and reverent: 'No one, Sir (or Lord)'. So Jesus has not opposed the law of Moses. She is liberated: without witnesses and without a confession there can be neither crime nor condemnation. There was no one there who was without sin. Or was there?

Jesus in his reply reveals what the woman did not know. 'Not even I (the one without sin), condemn you. There will be no stones thrown today.' She is freed from the possibility of condemnation twice — first by the hands of sinful men, then by Jesus' own sinless hands. They condemn, he does not. Clearly, he valued repentance and conversion more than just reprisal.

Maria Boulding perceptively comments, 'He has a sureness of touch… he has nothing to be afraid of in himself… he must have completely accepted and integrated his own sexuality. Only a man who has done so, or at least begun to do so, can relate properly to women.'[3]

Jesus commands her, 'Go!' She is no longer 'in the middle', she is not carted away as a lifeless corpse, but leaves of her own accord. But Jesus does not send her away because he thinks the charges against her are false. This is suggested by the phrase, 'from now on no longer continue in sin' (the Greek tense implies that this was something that occurred regularly). He offers her the power to take personal responsibility for her actions. He does not condemn, nor does he condone. He does not threaten her but offers her another chance in life. Does he even offer her the possibility that from now on she would be the one without sin?

In a sense, Jesus treated both the woman and the Jewish leaders in the same way: he offered them the power to take responsibility for their actions. Little did the scribes and Pharisees realise that by bringing the woman out into the open they themselves were about to be exposed as sinful in their collective heartlessness for her murder.

Jesus also will experience injustice. Some will be so infuriated with him in the temple that, ironically, the only one without sin is threatened with stones (8:59).

4. Where are we in the story?

Several traditional truths are suggested. Most fundamentally, that none of us is sinless. As 1 John reminds us, 'If we say that we haven't sinned, we are fooling ourselves and the truth isn't in our hearts' (1:9).

Certainly Jesus rejects violence, especially against women. After a decade of promoting the *Ecumenical decade for churches in solidarity with women* (1988–98), the World Council of Churches reported that violence is an experience which binds women together across every region and tradition, and that many women expect violence to be a part of their lives.[4] As Christians, we are surely following the example of Jesus when we work against this violence. Readers of the powerful novels *The Kite Runner* and *A Thousand Splendid Suns* by Khaled Hosseini will understand the appalling violence still perpetrated against women in some cultures.

This story also confirms that we should 'love the sinner but hate the sin'. In fact, most of us still find that a difficult balance to maintain. This woman represents all the people we may have relegated to the margins of society. Jesus' love is offered to all, regardless of their social status.

Every day we make the decisions to throw the first stone or to drop it and forgive. The angry crowd could have thrown that stone without a moment's notice because all they saw was the sin and not the person they were attacking. It is like some people who every day throw stones at a prostitute, a homosexual, a drug addict, or an alcoholic. Stone after stone they throw at these 'sins' and then one day their son or daughter comes to them and tells them that he or she is a prostitute, addicted to drugs, or a homosexual, or an alcoholic. They stand there with the stone in their hands but they can't throw the stone because now the 'sin' has a face, not any face, but their son's or daughter's face and they can't throw the rock.

It is one thing to discern between what is good and bad, but another to be judgemental. We are judgemental when we stop caring and praying for the person and simply pass on the bad news about them. It's one thing to say, 'That's wrong, stop it'. It's quite another to say, 'You're worthless because you did something wrong'. The first is a judgement. The second is judgementalism.

In the movie *Forest Gump*, there is a scene where Jenny has gone back to her childhood home and as she stands there looking at the shell of that old house memories flood her mind of what her father had done to her when she was a child. She kneels down, picks up a stone and throws it at a nearby window. Again and again she keeps throwing stones at the house, crying in frustration and in his simplistic way Forest Gump says, 'You know there's just never enough stones'.

You know there are never enough stones in life. I encourage you: drop your stones.

Some of us need to release the judgement we have been holding in our hearts towards other people or groups of people. Is there someone in your life that you need to forgive because they have wronged you? Is there someone you need to extend grace to because they are different from you or make you feel uncomfortable? Will you drop your stone and give it to God?

As a society we readily condemn athletes, politicians and those in the media. Like the Pharisees, the media and the crowd often throw stones without considering the evidence. Vigilante justice is all too frequently a pretext to grind some personal axe or express personal bias. Stones often hit their target and cause unnecessary damage. Let us drop our stones and encourage others to do the same.

Then some of us need to forgive ourselves, to release the judgement and condemnation we are placing on ourselves. Is there something that you have done in your past and you feel that you don't deserve grace, that no one can or should extend it to you? The truth is that God wants to extend that grace, he wants you to forgive yourself, release it to him and move forward. Go and sin no more.

Whether it is that you no longer live with judgement in your heart, or that you release yourself from judgement, or allow Jesus to heal the judgement: this is the encounter with Jesus that we all need.

We may drop our stones of hatred and of judgementalism at his feet and resolve to love as he has first loved us. Here we may hear the word of acceptance, 'Neither do I condemn you — go and sin no more'.

Discussion questions

1. Read section 1 (8:2).
   What are the elements of the situation that lead to the comment, 'all the more ironic'?

2. Read section 2 (8:3–6).
   - Look at Leviticus 20:10. 'Now in the law Moses commanded...' (8:5).
   - What do you think their selective use of the law suggests about the accusers? How can the Bible be used selectively today?

3. Read section 3 (8:6–9).
   'He manages both to recognise the Bible's teaching and at the same time to honour his own unique compassion.' In what ways has Jesus done both? What does it mean to describe Jesus as 'full of grace and truth' (1:17)?
   - Discuss the quotation from Maria Boulding beginning, 'He has a sureness of touch...'.

4. Read section 4.
   What are the ingredients in us that lead us to be often like the scribes and Pharisees, and to be less often like Jesus?
   - What is unleashed by standing in another person's shoes?
   - Reflect personally on why Jesus is saying to you, 'Neither do I condemn you — go and sin no more'.

1541-1614, Healing of the Man Born Blind, El Greco (Domenikos Theotokopoulos)

Chapter Six

'One thing I do know!'— Jesus and a blind man
(John 9:1–41)

Here is another of the biblical stories that offer us what one modern hymn calls 'glimpses of hope and visions of new birth', prompting the prayer, 'that we might see ourselves as we could be'.[1] This story is indeed about what we might see: a beautifully constructed narrative, full of rich irony, about blindness and seeing, the response side of darkness and light — a dominant theme in John.

Darkness is a stark symbolism even for those of us who enjoy sight. One of the ten plagues in Egypt was 'a darkness thick enough to be felt' (Exodus 10:21 *Good News Bible*). When novelist William Styron (*Sophie's Choice* and other novels) wrote about his lifetime struggles with depression, he used a phrase from Milton to call his 1990 book, *Darkness Visible: A Memoir of Madness*.[2] Styron could find no way to describe it other than to say it feels like a black cloud, a stifling darkness which is so vivid, so strong, as to block out all of life's light. In the throes of depression, nothing bright, nothing good, nothing happy can even reach a person. It feels that the person is sinking into a black pit or abyss.

So Jesus as Light of the World (8:12; 9:5) can speak to us at different levels of experience. This story shows precisely how Jesus is light.

The best way to understand this dramatic story is to see it as a set of scenes in which the characters interact. The blind man becomes a 'paradigm of growing discipleship',[3] even though it causes him a crisis of identity within his former community. In contrast, the Pharisees descend into a wilful state of disbelief and refuse to see what is before their eyes. They descend into darkness. As usual with John, we will find that we are ourselves inevitably drawn into the drama.

1. SCENE 1: Jesus and the disciples (9:1–5)

Jesus comes directly from the temple and sees this man. Presumably he was always there begging. Jesus stopped and gazed at him. This is a consoling truth about Jesus; he constantly notices the hurting people. This man could not see Jesus but Jesus saw him. His disciples mistake Jesus' intense looking and ask the question that they foolishly thought Jesus must have been thinking, a question that doubtlessly this poor man had often heard. 'Who sinned? This man or his parents?' (9:2).

This thoughtful poem was prompted by our story:

> Somehow, people who think of themselves as healthy and full of life,
> will talk about the sick,
> the disabled, the dying,
> and the mentally ill as objects rather than as persons.
> Just like the disciples of John 9:2.
> They chose to speak about the blind man
> rather than speak compassionately with him.
> Their very questions were degrading and dehumanizing.
> As though somehow his life had been judged

> to be of no value,
> to be a non-entity.
> But what is even worse than the isolation,
> is the expectation that the blind man
> would accept their condemnation
> and agree that he was so worthless that God would never heal him.[4]

Given the disciples' theological presuppositions, their reasoning was logical enough. God could not be the cause of evil. Being blind was surely an evil. It must, therefore, be the result of human sin. Who had sinned, the man's parents, or the man himself, even though he had been blind from birth? Punished for sins of the parents? The baby had sinned? In the womb? On the way to being born? The mind boggles.

Yet we still do it! The question of sin causing illness or catastrophe is not simply from the first century. We have all heard the question: 'What did I do to deserve this?'

Jesus cuts across all accepted explanations that wonder about human responsibility for suffering. He insists that it is an improper question. 'Because of his blindness you will see God work a miracle for him' (9:3, in the *Contemporary English Version*). This translation removes a potential problem of interpretation such as in the *New Revised Standard Version*: 'He was born blind so that God's works might be revealed in him'. That implies God is some kind of monster, condemning this poor man to long years of blindness so that one day Jesus could come along and show what God could do.

How was it that Jesus put it in the Sermon on the Mount? 'He [God] makes his sun rise on the evil and on the good, and sends rain on the righteous and on the unrighteous' (Matthew 5:45).

The little Greek word used in 9:3 (*hina*) could express purpose ('in order that') or it could express a result ('because of'). It could even be translated as an imperative: 'Let the works of God be displayed in him!' All this technical stuff is to say that this text does not require us to believe that God acts like a monster.

Our world is not perfect. Sometimes bad things happen because people make bad choices — we choose to sin. But it is also true that sometimes bad things 'just happen'. Innocent babies are born with big problems. Horrible accidents that are no one's fault seem to just happen. Yet all of us have known times when some really good things followed those 'bad things'. God somehow turns the bad into a blessing.

So Jesus affirms that, faced with the mystery of suffering, 'we' must be busy doing God's works. The disciples are associated with Jesus who is the light of the world shining in the darkness. We too must continue his work knowing that it is only ever the presence of Jesus that can bring light into our world.

2. SCENE 2: Jesus and the blind man (9:6–7)

Years of suffering, stigma and shame had made him who he is. The needy man has not begged Jesus to help as in many miracle stories. Spittle on the eyes evidently was a traditional practice in ancient times and Jesus puts mud on his eyes. When Jesus commands him to go and wash in the pool of Siloam he unquestioningly obeys. Four verbs show his obedience: he went, he washed, he came back, he saw. Accepting the word of Jesus, as we have already seen in John's stories, brings dramatic change.

This man did not deserve to be blind because he had sinned, and he did not deserve to be made well because he was good. Jesus took compassion on him; he simply obeyed, and a miracle took place — he could see! Siloam was a real pool but John links it with the revelation about Jesus: Siloam means 'sent' and Jesus was active as the one sent from God who now sends this man who had never seen light to his deliverance from darkness, just as he will for all who believe.

3. SCENE 3: The blind man and his neighbours(9:8–12)

What a wonderful detail in the story. Observers are confused. Is it really him? It looks like him! And he keeps on saying, 'It really is me!' Hoskyns observes, 'A sinner whose heart God has enlightened and changed by his grace is not easily known again. He is no longer the same man.'[5]

The healing does not lead to praise of God but to a division, to a crisis, to suspicions. They persevere with the question, 'How?' All he can say is that *a man named Jesus* did it.

4. SCENE 4: The blind man and the Pharisees (9:13–17)

These neighbours cart the blind man off to those who should be able to sort all this out, the people who know their Bibles, the religious elite. But as John warns us (9:14), it was the Sabbath when Jesus put mud in the blind man's eyes. (Look back at chapter 5 in John to see why John tells us this: Jesus had healed a paralytic on the Sabbath and the Pharisees had been furious.)

A further division erupts. Controversies leave no room for celebrations. Some of the Pharisees immediately saw an answer. If Jesus had done this on the Sabbath, clearly he was not from God. Why not? Because the Sabbath was from God, it was his special gift to his people. To 'work' on the Sabbath was to break Jewish law — no question about that! Clearly then, he was a sinner. But at least some of the Pharisees saw the problem: how could a sinner do something like this? Their real problem was the preservation of their legal tradition; they could not celebrate with the blind man.

So the rather confused and startled man is addressed. 'Well, it was your eyes that are causing this problem! What do you say about him?' The man moves up one step in his understanding of Jesus: from being a *man* Jesus is now called a *prophet* (9:17). New vision leads to a new courage in giving witness. The man is growing in the light, whilst the Pharisees, we will discover, are still stumbling in the dark.

5. SCENE 5: The blind man and his parents (9:18–23)

So they just wanted 'the facts'. Belief is beyond them. Perhaps the man wasn't really blind, at least not from the beginning of his life? So the parents are called up. John explains that they were terrified, not because they had sensed God's mysterious power in their midst, but because the Jewish leaders had made it clear that Jesus was not from God and anyone who dared confess him as Messiah would be cast out of the synagogue. They did not want that and so simply rehearsed the sad story of their son's life up to this point, and said, 'Well, you ask him!' His new sight has brought immediate responsibilities and a peculiar isolation.

Perhaps the reaction of the parents is the saddest part of this story. Fear makes cowards of us all. This exchange has not advanced the Pharisees' quest at all and their anger burns through this story.

6. SCENE 6: The Pharisees and the blind man (9:24–34)

So the blind man is called back. When his eyes were opened he saw a hostile world all around him. The level of scrutiny is ludicrous. Obsession with observance is a characteristic of a dangerous religion, as many forms of fundamentalism have shown. Like sadistic torturers, they press for the confession that they just know must be the truth. The alternative is too much to contemplate.

He is asked to take an oath. But the God they want the man to 'glorify' is a god of their own imagining, not the God of Jesus. They just know that Jesus must be a sinner. The blind man (finally) loses patience, 'I don't know about that. *But I will tell you what I do know!* A few hours ago I could not see one solitary thing, but now I see light. I have my sight. I can see you! *That is the one thing that I really know!*'

They are not persuaded even by the logic of this testimony. They are obsessed with the 'how' question rather than the 'who' question. What did he do? They press him and then in a wonderfully ironic touch, the man says, 'I have told you. Do you want to hear it all over again? Perhaps you too want to become his disciples!'

I like this man! They protest that they are disciples of Moses but not 'this fellow, Jesus'. *Where does he come from?* The question of the whole gospel haunts them and even this healed and excited man cannot shake them from their cherished traditions. Incredibly, 'Moses' has become their blind spot! They look back to what was, rather than opening their eyes to see what is now happening. God's word is limited and contained by their expert knowledge.

The healed man debates with them: never since creation has anyone opened the eyes of the blind. Indeed! Readers of John know that this living Word, Jesus, was there at the beginning and without him not one thing came into being (1:1). The man has grown even further towards the Light. He now knows that something new has entered the human story. But they retreat into the darkness of unbelief and throw him out; how dare he, 'a sinner since the day he was born', lecture them on God and what God does in the world.

7. SCENE 7: Jesus and the blind man (9:35–38)

The man has not yet even seen Jesus. But Jesus, as always, seeks and finds the one who is rejected and thrown out by the religious elite. He asks for a commitment of faith. This is a crisis point in the story. The man responds, 'Lord, I put my faith in you!' When Jesus speaks, he is seen and known. The healed man now has the full gift of sight; he not only sees but he sees *Jesus*.

The man now believes. Doubted by friends and neighbours, abandoned by his parents, questioned, insulted and cast out by Jewish leaders, he has stumbled from belief in Jesus as a man, to Jesus as a prophet (one called by God). With this recognition that Jesus must be 'from God', the once blind man now finally prostrates himself before the one who makes God known, the Son of Man, the Sent one, the Light of the World.

8. SCENE 8: Jesus and the Pharisees (9: 39–41, though it extends into chapter 10)

Jesus' words drip with irony. 'I came into this world for judgment so that those who do not see may see, and those who do see may become blind' (9:39). The arrogance of those who tell Jesus that they can see is neatly turned back to the opening question: If you were blind you would not have sinned.

Perhaps that had been shown every day as they had walked past that blind man. He sat and begged there daily, and every day they walked by him, but when the time came, they couldn't be sure of who he was; others had to fetch his parents before they could be sure of the identification. They had never really looked at him, as Jesus did. But now they kept on saying, 'We see'; and Jesus adds, 'So you remain in sin' (9:40–41).

Clearly, the blind man is the central character in this precious narrative. His experience of God is an extreme dislocation from his previous life. Step by step, he is taken out of himself. When his eyes were opened, the world had grown hostile to him. When Jesus finds him he is isolated from the community of neighbours, family and religious authorities. When the whole fabric of his former identity seems to have been torn apart, the moment of revelation occurs. He says, 'Lord, I believe', and worships him. The man was brought into a new identity and a new world of relationships. His only security now is in surrender to this One. He has passed from a life of humiliation to a bold and unashamed testimony: 'One thing I do know' has grown into the confession, 'My Lord and God'.

Once again, we must each ask ourselves: where do I fit into this story? Have we seen ourselves as we could be? Am I among the undecided neighbours? Am I a member of a religious authority, preventing the truth about God being spoken? Am I among the disciples who wish endlessly to discuss the human condition? Am I with the frightened and uninvolved parents, scared of what it might cost me to receive what Christ has done in our world? Am I the man born blind, sitting on the margins, ready to see Jesus in my life, and to tell others that I have? Maybe, even, I am like Jesus, intentionally seeking the marginalised and the outcast, expecting and praying they'll show me something of the truth of God.

The truth is, we are all of those characters. With each one of us, God reaches past the parts of us we think are the most presentable. God reaches through these into our brokenness, the parts of ourselves we hide for fear others wouldn't love us or like us if they knew it. God reaches there, and makes it a place of healing and transformation. God does not want our best parts. God wants it all. God uses the places in our lives where we feel the most vulnerable and the most broken. God enters into our brokenness and, in those places, offers hope, and healing, and transformation.

We love to sing this song:

> Amazing grace! How sweet the sound
> that saved a wretch like me!
> I once was lost, but now am found,
> was blind but now I see.

Well, what do you see?

Discussion questions

1. How does this story help us to 'see ourselves as we might be'?

2. Read scene 1 (9:1–5).
   What are some of the sources and dangers of stereotyping people? Can you think of modern examples of ways that we do this?
   Discuss the poem beginning, 'Somehow people who think of themselves…'.
   What would you say to someone who told you that they believed God was punishing them because of something bad that they had done?

3. Read Scene 2: (9:6–7).
   What response was needed to elicit such a dramatic change in the blind man?

4. Read Scene 3: (9:8–12).
   Why can we all 'wear' the T-shirt stating 'I am a work in progress'?

5. Scene 4: (9:13–17).
   What are the underlying issues in the contrasts that John presents?

6. Read Scene 5: (9:18–23).
   What differences are there between 'religion' and 'knowing Jesus'?

7. Read Scene 6: (9:24–34).
   Discuss ways in which religious tradition may promote 'blindness'.

8. Read Scene 7: (9:35–38).
   What makes this passage the 'crisis point'?

9. Read Scene 8: (9:39–41).
   - In what ways can you identify with the experience of the blind man 'when his eyes were opened'?
   - Jesus presents himself as 'the Light of the World'. What has his light done in your life?

1303-1305, The Resurrection of Lazarus, Giotto

Chapter Seven

'If only you had been here!' —
Jesus and a grieving family
(John 11:1–46)

Across the ages the dramatic story of the resurrection of Lazarus has fascinated artists, musicians and poets. It is still attracting attention. My 'search engine' advises me that there are at least seven pop bands which are called 'Lazarus' but I am not sure why this should be! 'Lazarus' has, of course, become a metaphor for those who experience some form of significant renewal in their life. Former Australian Prime Minister John Howard called his memoirs *Lazarus Rising* as a way of underlining the revival of his seemingly dead political career.[1]

But there are more significant reasons why this story about Lazarus deserves our careful attention. Here are some of the most loved words in the New

Testament: 'I am the resurrection and the life. Those who believe in me, even though they die, will live, and everyone who lives and believes in me will never die' (11:25–26). Christians trust this claim and promise of Jesus — we recite these words at funerals and turn to them at times of loss. What could be more relevant for us as we are forced to face the inevitability of our own death and mourn the loss of loved ones?

The remarkable story of the resurrection of Lazarus is offered to us as historical record, but also calls us to faith. It is another of the stories about encounters with Jesus in John's Gospel that leads people to confront their own lives and can also help us discover who Jesus is and how he can transform us.

True, this story bristles with problems of interpretation apart from the central miracle of someone being raised from the dead. How can we understand the delay of Jesus in going to the grieving family? We are comforted to learn that Jesus wept, but why was he so angry and upset (which is the implication of the word for 'greatly disturbed' in 11:33)?

As we consider these questions let us note two basic truths from this story.

1. The story is a sign of God's love and glory

John's account of the raising of Lazarus is one of several sign stories in this gospel. As we have seen, a sign story consists of a miraculous act of Jesus usually surrounded or followed by a theological discussion of its meaning. Examples are John's presentation of Jesus turning water to wine, healing a cripple at the pool, and giving sight to a man born blind. The raising of Lazarus is the climactic and most miraculous episode in the series of signs.

At least two features mark sign stories. First, Jesus acts according to his own time and not according to external pressures. For example, Jesus separates himself from his mother (2:4) before acting at the wedding feast at Cana. We should not, then, be disturbed by Jesus' response to the urgent message about Lazarus's illness (11:3–6).

Visiting the bereaved is an important aspect of Jewish piety and the delay could appear to dishonour the family, but Jesus stayed where he was for two more days.

This was not, as some have suggested, simply to ensure that Lazarus was truly dead. He certainly did not wait so that the miracle would seem greater!

No, the work of Jesus has its own hour. As Frank Moloney puts it, 'The motivation for Jesus' decision to go to Bethany is a response to God's designs, not to human need'. The real crisis Jesus is confronting is not the family crisis in Bethany, but the crisis of the world; not the death of Lazarus, but his own death (as is hinted at in 11:8, 16).

Second, to say this is a sign story means that its primary function is revelation. Some truth about the meaning of God's glory and presence in the world is conveyed through this miracle. These stories must be seen to operate on two levels. On one level Jesus heals a cripple, opens the eyes of the blind or raises the dead; but on another level a truth about the eternal life that Jesus brings is revealed.

A key verse is: 'When Jesus got the message, he said, "This sickness is not fatal. It will become an occasion to show God's glory by glorifying God's Son"'(11: 4).[2]

In one way, Jesus is glorified by the resurrection of Lazarus. In another way, the hour of Jesus' glory is his suffering and death (John 12:23; 13:31; 17:1). Lazarus's sickness (and resurrection) is for the glory of God not just because of itself, but because it will ultimately lead to Jesus' death. The chapter concludes with the Jews conspiring to kill Jesus. One death leads to the other. By a cruel irony, Jesus will be put to death because he brought Lazarus back to life.

Of course this was at the same time an act of love. The Bethany family and the unnamed 'disciple whom Jesus loved' are the only individuals in John whom Jesus is specifically said to love (11:5). (Some have suggested that Lazarus was this beloved disciple.)

So this story is also about what it means to be in relationship with Jesus, what it means to love him and be loved by him. Love is linked inextricably to death in John: 'No one has greater love than this' (15:13) and that is also true in the story of this family.

Out of love, Jesus does not go to his loved ones. Their relationship with Jesus does not mean that sad things do not happen. He does not prevent Lazarus from dying. But he is ultimately present to them, and God is glorified even in something that feels so painful. The story then is a sign of God's glory and love.

2. The story is a source of faith and hope

We may find ourselves in this story.

Lazarus is us. Actually Lazarus is a rather passive and silent figure in the story; the sisters do the talking but of course the miracle directly affected him. John repeatedly uses the physical realm as a metaphorical pointer to the spiritual realm. Water is a metaphor for the quenching of our spiritual thirst through Jesus' presence — Jesus is the living water (4:14). The bread Jesus multiplies to feed the crowd is a metaphor for the satisfaction of our spiritual hunger that Jesus brings; Jesus is the Bread from Heaven (6:35). Here, in chapter 11, the restoration of physical life is a metaphor for breaking free from the bonds of spiritual death into the gift of eternal life that Jesus brings. Jesus is the resurrection and the life. So we, like Lazarus, need this miracle of resurrection.

The disciples are us. In so much of John's Gospel, words in conversations with Jesus are misunderstood and a deeper meaning lies beneath the surface, as with the discussion about Lazarus 'sleeping' (11:11–14), ending with the startling words, 'I am glad I was not there!' So we, too, seem to stumble in the dark as we so often struggle to understand what Jesus is doing in our world.

Martha is us. In her grief she turns to Jesus. 'Lord, if you had been here, my brother would not have died. But even now I know that God will give you whatever you ask of him' (11:21–22). Is this an accusation as well as an affirmation of faith? Jesus replies with a simple affirmation, 'Your brother will rise again' (11:23). She thinks that this is simply standard Jewish (Pharisaic) belief about a general resurrection at the last day (11:24).

But Jesus takes her beyond this to focus on the meaning of his coming with those memorable words beginning, 'I am the resurrection and the life' (11:25–26). Yes, they will be raised up at the end (see 6:54) but they have life now. Those who have the Son, have life. This story, though not simply a parable, is also a dramatic representation of this great truth: to believe in Jesus is to pass from death to life.

The Resurrection and the Life! He does not say he will *give* these. He *is* these. Resurrection is no longer a pious hope or a controversial dogma. Resurrection now has 'a living face and a name'.[3]

What does this mean? Is not resurrection to life enough (so some Greek manuscripts omit 'and life')? It is one of the 'I AM' sayings that point us to the deity of Christ. How is he resurrection? Simply, fellowship with him is sharing in the divine life now as well as at the end of our life. In baptism, do we not confess that we have moved from death to life? It is about a special quality of existence in the here and now that comes to all who have faith in him. Martha confesses her belief in Jesus as the Messiah and the Son of God (11:27).

Yet she falters when Jesus is before the tomb. She has not fully grasped what has been said. She makes the natural observation that after four days the smell will be intolerable. Jesus' reply harks back to the need for faith to see the glory of God.

Mary is us. She weeps in her humanity as Easterners traditionally have done, with loud wailing and intense grief. Out of the depths of her pain she cries to Jesus. So we cry in our experiences of pain and loss. If only you had been here! Where is God when we need him?

But Jesus heard them and God hears us. When Jesus seems slow in coming he is coming nonetheless. With Jesus it is never too late for there is no loss that can separate us from him. As James Baldwin wrote in *The Fire Next Time*, 'The Lord never seems to get there when you want him, but when he arrives he's always right on time'.[4] We may bring all our anger, disappointment, anguish, perplexity and anxiety to him. He weeps with us.

Why did Jesus respond the way he did, 'greatly disturbed and deeply moved' (11:33)? Jesus is experiencing something like a 'Gethsemane'; he knows that calling Lazarus out of the tomb means that he must enter it. Soon the story will be told — the Jews plot, the cross looms. There is no other way because only in this act can God be glorified and the resurrection and the life come to the world that God so loves. In and through the Lazarus story we surely see the Jesus story — the tomb, the stone rolled away, the women close by, the grave clothes. Sound familiar?

Campbell Morgan wrote powerfully, 'He made himself responsible, and gathered up into his own personality all the misery resulting from sin, represented in a dead man and broken-hearted people round about him… It is a most remarkable unveiling of the heart of Jesus'.[5]

Lazarus is commanded to come out. With an eyewitness touch we are told that he was bound up — perhaps he almost tripped. So Jesus says, unbind him and let him go.

Lazarus is us, bound by death in our current lives, called to life by Jesus who is the Light and the Life of the world. Jesus stands at the edge of our tomb, shouting 'Come out!' We are to substitute our own name for that of Lazarus, hear his command, and walk into the light of day, pulling free of our grave clothes as we go.

Mary, Martha and Lazarus are not simply props for this story. They are real people facing death and experiencing grief but they witness the coming of the Word of life into the world.

The story of Lazarus catches death in the moment of its transformation. Faith is summoned to such a point of conviction that death appears incidental to Christian existence, in view of the endless life that has already begun. Jesus gives life by moving closer to what is yet to take place — his own death. His power to vanquish death is not exercised from the outside, as it were, at no cost to himself — he acts from within.[6]

No, this miracle was not simply for certain people who had the great benefit of living there at the same time as Jesus, when water was changed into wine, when the blind saw, when the dead were raised. True faith does not distinguish between our being there or his being here. Faith begins with us where we are.

Robert McAfee Brown, an American theologian of a generation or two ago, wrote about how this story changed one man's life. Brown was an army chaplain on a troopship bringing back marines from Japan for discharge after World War II. He was asked by a small group to lead Bible studies and towards the end of their trip they read this passage. After they had studied it one marine came to him. 'Everything in that chapter is pointing at me.' He told the chaplain how he had been in a kind of hell for the last six months. He had got into trouble, made a mess of his life, though nobody knew much about it. He felt guilty and that his life was ruined. He felt as though he was a dead man. 'After reading this chapter, I have come alive again. I know that this resurrection Jesus was talking about is real here and now, for he has raised me from death to life.'[7]

That is it. Jesus is the Resurrection and the Life. Jesus asks the same question of us that he asked of Martha, 'Do you believe this? Do you believe that I am the resurrection and the life? Do you believe that I not only offer you resurrection in the future but also fullness of life now in the present?'

Jesus proclaims that he is both the *resurrection* and the *life*. It is an invitation from Jesus to enter into the fullness of his life in the present, right now, and that life will continue in us after death. Let us accept Jesus' invitation, walk out of our tomb and allow ourselves to be unbound and really live.

Discussion questions

1. Read: 'The story is a sign of God's love and glory'.
    - What is meant by, 'In one way, Jesus is glorified by the resurrection of Lazarus. In another way, the hour of Jesus' glory is his suffering and death'?
    - How does the Lazarus story show 'what it means to be in relationship with Jesus, what it means to love him and be loved by him'?

2. Read: 'The story is a source of faith and hope'.
    - In what ways do you identify with Lazarus, the disciples, Martha, Mary?
    - What does it mean to you that Jesus is 'the Resurrection and the Life'?
    - Why could Campbell Morgan write of the Lazarus story, 'It is a most remarkable unveiling of the heart of Jesus'?

1874, Jesus Anointing, Alexander Bida

Chapter Eight

'Smell the waste!' —
Jesus and a woman who loves him
(John 12:1–8)

Rudyard Kipling once claimed that 'smells are surer than sounds or sights to make your heartstrings crack'.[1] So this story would suggest. Here is a story of loving extravagance that in one form or another is in all four gospels. The way that John tells it is memorable because he was clearly there and, as he wrote, he remembered the aromatic fragrance that had wafted through the whole house.

That simple dwelling at Bethany where Mary, Martha and Lazarus lived had become something of a home for Jesus and his disciples. Many of us recall not only the sounds and sights of home but the special smells, perhaps of a Sunday roast dinner cooking! John's heartstrings surely cracked as he recalled that never-to-be-forgotten meal, and especially that haunting aroma.

It was the beginning of that tumultuous week. 'Six days before the Passover' (12:1), the Saturday evening of the week that was to change the course of history. Crowds were gathering in Jerusalem; Jesus had withdrawn to a tiny town near the desert for a quiet space with his disciples (11:54–57). People were abuzz with excitement.

After all, Jesus had just performed an extraordinary miracle, the raising from the dead of his friend Lazarus (11:1–44). This had strengthened the Jewish leaders in their determination to kill Jesus and Lazarus as well.

As John in a simple sentence tells us, the crowds were gathering in the temple and asking, 'He won't come here. Will he? Surely not!' (11:56). The hunt for Jesus was on and this most significant week was about to unfold.

As we read this story, then, we must not miss the timing. The imminent death of Jesus dominates these events of chapters 11 and 12. Jesus quietly arrives at Bethany, probably with all 12 disciples. Martha is not fazed this time (recall the story in Luke 10) and serves a possible total of 17 with evident equanimity.

What a conversation they must have had, Jesus and Lazarus together! What did Lazarus look like? 'How are you feeling?' becomes more than a polite inquiry. Were there even questions about what it was like to die? Our imagination must be contained. Something much more important is about to happen.

Mary perhaps was the first to understand where all these events were leading and she somehow sensed that her precious friend and Lord was soon to be killed. Had she planned this extraordinary act? Surely not — it all seems so spontaneous and unexpected. She had bought and kept this rich treasure. Judas was the bean counter and his estimate was likely to be extremely accurate — he was good at these things — and he said it was worth 300 denarii, say, a year's wages for a working man! Had she kept it for the anointing of Lazarus? Was it something special she had kept for personal use?

And what does Mary do with it? Before the astonished gasp of everyone, she takes this expensive bottle of perfume and pours it, all of it, over the feet of Jesus. Then she does what was even more unthinkable. In a home, but before a man not her husband (indeed before several such men), she undoes her hair and wipes off the ointment with her hair. Mary's love floods the house with fragrance. John remembers, 'the sweet smell of the perfume filled the house'.

The rabbis had a saying, 'The scent of good oil is diffused from the bedchamber to the dining hall while a good name is diffused from one end of the world to the other'. Knowing John's love of symbolism, this is perhaps his way of telling us what Mark says in his account (14:9), 'Wherever the good news is told all over the world, people will remember what she's done'.

There are three main characters in this beautiful story: Mary, Judas and Jesus. Once again, a story from John involves us and asks how we will respond to Jesus.

1. Mary shows us how extravagant love is expressed towards Jesus

How can we understand what she did? Perhaps she didn't understand herself; this was a sudden impulse, not a calculated act. What did she mean?

Scholars have debated this. What was the meaning of the anointing? Some few think it was intended as a kind of royal anointing — after all, the next day Jesus rides into Jerusalem, a king on a donkey. But there is really no hint in John's text that this was her intention. In any case, it is the head of a king that is anointed and that invariably by a male!

Simple everyday courtesy suggests that a guest would be greeted with an anointing, but not a whole bottle and not on the feet! Why the feet? This is strange and most probably is to be understood as an act of genuine but abject humility; wiping the feet is the task of a slave — and she wipes with her own hair!

This is an act of unlimited devotion. Readers of this gospel will remember this when later in the week Jesus kneels before his disciples and washes their feet, a parable that as a humble servant he will serve the world (13:1–11).

So, why then? We will see how Jesus interprets her action but perhaps she didn't herself know why! It was simply *an act of extravagant love*, selfless, purely sensual, uncalculating, an overwhelming sense that this dear man's life is in danger. Her astonishing generosity reveals her great love.

Elizabeth Moltmann-Wendel has suggested that what Mary does comes from the depths of her personality.[2] She may not be good with words but what she does without speaking and yet with astonishing self-confidence has a spontaneous effect. The sweetness of her action is evident everywhere. All the elemental ways of showing her love for Jesus — respect, affection, tenderness, tears — are now released with the fragrant oil.

As Moltmann observes, this servile task is one that is incomprehensible to many women today. She does what no man would have done and we suspect what Martha would never have done — we can imagine Martha as dumbfounded as anyone else. Dear sweet, quiet sitting-at-the feet-of-Jesus Mary!

But it is *her* idea, *her* way of showing love. 'It is her revolution.' She has come out of the shadows to be herself. This is who she is! This is her faith, her love. Even if it means she will do the unconventional or go beyond accepted ways of conduct.

Mary shows the revolutionary potential of love. 'Mary has a face of her own, the face of many women. But she begins a history of her own which has no parallels, except perhaps in the history of women who discover that the gospel does not suppress their individuality but develops it, and amounts to the adventure of being themselves.'[3]

2. Judas shows a calculating hypocrisy towards this act of love

Imagine the stunned silence after Mary's generous and breathtaking act of love. Those of us older, undemonstrative and usually unsentimental Aussie males are similarly alarmed by any spontaneous and emotional act like this.

Finally one of the men, a leader of the disciples — such a leader as to be trusted with the gifts that some richer friends gave them to help keep Jesus and the little group with food and clothing — cannot contain his anger. 'Why was this perfume not sold and the money given to the poor?'

The smell was too much for Judas Iscariot. 'Just smell the waste!' Her spendthrift and eccentric attitude aroused his wrath. Encased in his own selfishness he objected to the selfless extravagance of Mary's gesture. What could be done to help the poor with money like that! Was he the only one there to think like this? Whether it was for the poor or for himself, 300 denarii have their own aroma, for good or for ill.

But this story is not only about love, but also about hypocrisy. Her generosity is set against his avarice, his pettiness against her large heartedness. 'To the worldly mind', says William Temple, 'acts of devotion are always foolish'.[4] Her gift was unspeakably precious to Jesus.

We cannot leave Judas without a word of regret. Judas had a point, as often those who are versed in financial matters do. (Some of my best friends are accountants and we all need their help!) Caring about the poor meant caring about the bottom line. We will be listening for what Jesus has to say about this.

But here the stress is rather on Judas's hypocrisy: he did not care about the poor but his own profit. He was not the last financier in church circles to be tempted. He must have had a gift for handling money and his temptation came at his point of ability. That is usually how we all are tempted and when we are given trust, it can lead to a fall.

His fate is a great tragedy — to be one of the chosen twelve and yet to be the one who is both a traitor and a thief. He is a melancholy reminder that even proximity to Jesus and his followers is no guarantee against failure when our hearts are consumed with arrogance and greed.

3. Jesus accepts love and rebukes hypocrisy

Jesus responds quickly and decisively. 'Leave her alone!' (12:7–8). He insists that she has understood the significance of what is happening. She had recently prepared her brother's body for burial and now deep in her inner being senses she must do the same for Jesus. Her action is 'a symbolical embalming of his body for burial, as though he were already dead'.[5] The cross is a shadow in the room. Yes, the Bible does say 'you will always have the poor with you' (Deuteronomy 15:11), but this once-for-all event is even more important! She has seized the moment whilst it was there.

Have you not sometimes wished that you could have a moment over again? A loved one dies and then at the funeral we say what the loved one never heard from

Chapter Eight

us about our love and respect! Some things we will never do unless we grasp the chance to do them when they come. So here, the time for showing love is almost gone. Mary has seized the moment in an unforgettable way.

Did she intend to show all that Jesus explained? Probably not. In John, words and deeds often have meaning beyond the intentions of those who speak and act. Caiaphas, the high priest, said to the council, 'It is better for you to have one man die for the people' (11:50). He was thinking and acting politically, but now we consider the greater truth of his words. When Jesus gave his life on the cross, he — one man — gave up his life so that all might be saved. That's not even close to what Caiaphas meant, but that is what happened.

At one point the Pharisees exclaimed, 'Look how the whole world has gone after him!' (12:19 NIV). They had no idea. For them, it was simply an exaggerated expression that revealed their astonishment at Jesus' great popularity. Now, indeed, the whole world does know the name of Jesus.

We speak and act in ways we think most appropriate for the occasion. But at the time, we may not know what power and what impact they carry in the hearts and minds of those who hear our words and see our deeds. To you, at the time you do it, it may be just a drink of cold water to someone who is thirsty. But to that person, it is the very source of life. There is life; there is power in the simplest deed if it is done to bring honour to Christ even if sometimes that may not be our direct intention.

That is what Mary has done. But, on second thought, it could be that she was the only one — or one of a few — who were aware that Jesus was about to go to the cross. Maybe she was the only one who really understood because she was willing to listen to Jesus with an open heart and mind.

Yes, we do still have the poor with us. And it would be all too easy for us to use this text as a justification for lavish spending on our churches or ourselves and ignore the needs of the world. But that would be hypocrisy as great as that of Judas, for the teaching of Jesus as well as his life shows clearly just how much we are called to live for others and to serve a needy world. Deuteronomy 15:11 notes that there will never cease to be some in need on the earth but it adds, 'Open your hand to the poor and needy neighbour'.

Moloney notes the link between the selfishness of Judas and the continual presence of the poor. 'Endemic to human society is the truth that the former creates the latter.'[6]

What then are we to make of this story? Mary had no idea her action would be remembered forever. She simply knew she wanted to show Jesus how much she loved him. So she gave to him, freely, without reservation or thought of cost. And now the whole world knows of it.

Love is like that. It just happens. When love calculates, love loses. When commitment requires a balance sheet, Judas wins; Jesus loses.

I don't know precisely what it might mean for you and me to love Jesus in a similar way. We do not touch Jesus' feet; we may not cry and wet his feet with our tears; our head may be bald; and we wouldn't throw away our annual wage by pouring some expensive perfume on a picture of a dying Christ.

So, how can we be like that woman in the story? Her life had been deeply touched by Jesus, so much so that she wanted to do something precious for Jesus. Can that be possible for us? That is, can our lives be so deeply touched by the living Christ that we want to respond in some special way?

Those of us who are Christians do. Each of us, having been deeply touched by Jesus, wants to respond to him and give our lives to him.

How do you respond to Christ so that Christ knows how you feel and that you appreciate all that he has done for you? Is our imagination so paralysed that we cannot think how we might show our love for Jesus? Whatever it may be, let us give to him freely, gladly. Gratitude is always at the heart of all true spirituality.

Maybe the Judas who lurks in our hearts needs to be quietened when we see the extravagant giving of others to Jesus. Are we too cynical, too old, and too tired not to be moved by the willing and extravagant pouring out of devotion to Jesus by some younger ones in our midst? 'Smell the waste. Think what you could make for yourself if you concentrated on your career and forgot about Jesus and his sacrifice for us!'

Chapter Eight

In my church a little while ago we were greatly moved by an old man, a member of our church for many years, named Eugene Veith, unsteady on his feet but quietly witnessing to us about how he had poured out his company's earnings to Jesus and people in need. He founded Veith transport (later sold to Mayne Nickless) and gave at least $23 million to religious and charity works. Bald, but known as 'Curly', Eugene founded Mission Enterprises and helped mission work around the world.[7] Eugene has now died but he is still spoken of with love as his mission work continues. I have no doubt he is in the presence of the One whom he loved with what seemed to others a foolish extravagance.

'Smell the waste!' business competitors would murmur. Jesus says, 'Leave him alone! He is doing it because he loves me!'

What can you smell in the air here today where you are? Is it the sourness of a greedy Judas? Pray God it is not so! Or can you smell the sweet waste — as ordinary men and women like us, in ways that we don't quite understand and which surprise us, pour out their lives and in gratitude shamelessly adore Jesus. Pray God that it will be so!

Discussion questions

Read section 1.
- What are the salient details of the timing of this scene?
- Which interpretations of the reasons for Mary's action in this scene do you favour?

1. Read section 2.
    - John does not mince his words about Judas (12:4 & 6). With Judas (one of the chosen 12!) in mind, how might 1 Corinthians 10:12–13 speak to you?

2. Read section 3.
    - Are you aware of examples of the following: 'There is life; there is power in the simplest deed if it is done to bring honour to Christ even if sometimes that may not be our direct intention'?
    - What are some of the elements that underlie, 'Gratitude is always at the heart of all true spirituality'?
    - Can you share experiences or examples of 'extravagant waste' in the service of Christ?

1304-1306, Jesus Washes the Feet of the Apostles, Giotto (Ambrogio Bondone)

Chapter Nine

'Do what I have done!' —
Jesus and confused friends
(John 13:1–20)

Most of us dread farewells. To stand at the airport and tearfully say goodbye to a loved one can be an ordeal. Even more, it is demanding to bid farewell to a loved one who is dying even though that can be a healing and rewarding experience. In earlier ages, the last words of a dying person were studiously recorded and in the Victorian era sentimental deathbed scenes were a common feature in religious magazines.

Reading this story we are reminded that this was a farewell scene. How could the disciples, and the later church for that matter, cope with the departure — the death — of Jesus? That is the theme of John chapters 13 to 17. Jesus knew his 'hour' had come (13:1). John had prepared readers for this. In 12:27 Jesus was troubled in his soul but insisted that this was why he came into the world, for the hour when God would glorify the Son and the Son would glorify the Father through his death (12:24–28). At the wedding in Cana he had told his mother that his hour had not come (2:4), but now it is here.

But if Jesus was burdened with this consciousness his friends seem to have scarcely realised what was ahead, even though Jesus had warned them. Craddock suggests that the disciples had been like children playing on the floor, only to look up and see their parents putting on coats and hats. There are three questions: Where are you going? Can we go too? Then who is going to stay with us?[1] These are the themes of the teaching of Jesus in the upper room. By example and words he prepares them for his imminent departure.

So this is an encounter with Jesus of a different order. The disciples have been with him for some time but they are about to be challenged in a new and startling way. The exciting days of walking with him, hearing his stories and insights into what he called God's kingdom, seeing amazing miracles and the enjoyment of simply being together with him, are about to come to a bewildering and terrifying end. For them then, and for us today, here are significant truths to be understood and obeyed on the way to a fuller grasp of what faith in Jesus means.

1. Jesus and his hour (13:1–2)

The central figure clearly is Jesus. We must remember that this is the week of the passion that began with the entry into Jerusalem (12:12–19). 'Here comes our king', the crowds had shouted as they waved their hastily gathered palms. Jesus meant them to see this incident with their king riding into the city on a young donkey as the fulfilment of God's ancient promise to his people. This was a symbol of both royalty and humility. As Graham Kendrick's popular hymn has it, Jesus combines 'meekness and majesty'.[2] Any Romans who might have chanced upon this scene would have laughed, as indeed they did later in the week: 'Behold your King!' they mocked as they paraded a pathetic and vulnerable looking victim of their cruelty. Pilate pressed a reluctant Jesus, 'Are you a King?' Is this some joke king, like a laughing King of Moomba in Melbourne? No, the Jesus of John's

Gospel is a king in a way that they did not understand: he is in control.

John tells us what Jesus knew, who he loved and what he did at that fateful hour.

What did he know? He knew that his hour had come (13:1). His death is not an accident. This is the design of God. Now is the time that he is to 'depart from this world and go to the Father'. Yes, Judas has a role to play. Yes, those who plot against him have a part. Pilate has his own confused destiny. But Jesus knows that what is to happen is God's purpose.

If you knew you were going to die very soon it would concentrate your mind! Priorities would be reviewed. What are the important things for Jesus? This story tells us. For Jesus it meant — wait for it! — washing the smelly feet of his friends!

But Jesus knew even more. The dazzling light of the truth is spelled out: 'Jesus,[knew] that the Father had given all things into his hands, and that he had come from God and was going to God' (13:3). What did this one do? Does he command the sun to stop or tell the angels to sing a song to his disciples? No, he stands up, dons an apron and pours water into a basin. Can you hear the sound of it? Can you see the hush and the confusion on the faces of the others? What does he do? He washes the feet of his disciples!

As Severian of Gabala preached on this passage (around 400 CE):

> He who wraps the heavens in clouds wrapped round himself a towel. He who pours the water into rivers and pools tipped… water into a basin. And he who before whom every knee bends in heaven and on earth and under the earth knelt to wash the feet of his disciples.[3]

He knew yet more. He knew that one of these startled friends at the table was about to betray him. Here in that holy place is the mystery of evil. The devil is a part of this awful scenario: 'The devil had already put it into the heart of Judas… to betray him' (13:2). Judas had welcomed this awful intruder. Jesus knew who was to betray him (13:11). So when Jesus gives Judas a morsel of bread dipped in a tasty sauce he tells him, 'Do quickly what you are going to do' (13:27). For whatever reason, and innumerable guesses have been made as to the motives of Judas, he is responsible for this foul deed. So with his feet still damp, still chewing on the morsel of bread, he goes away from that lit room and that friend. John simply adds, 'And it was night' (13:30). He was not telling us the time but the nature of the act.

We think we are smart. We laugh at the idea of the devil as we might at some imaginary 'bogey-man' who scares the kids. But Jesus knew Judas and he knows the devil. Evil is personal. We are responsible for what we do and yet there come times when something, some force drives us to act in ways that we regret and which do great harm to others.

There is no easy answer to the mystery of evil but Jesus and the Bible more generally teach us both to accept personal responsibility for what we do and to affirm the power of evil at work in our world. Jesus knew about that in that upper room.

His hour had come. Evil would now do its worst — Judas, and the Jews, and the Romans, and the devil! But Jesus knew that he was going to God. The hour had come.

2. Jesus and his disciples (13:4–20)

John not only tells us what Jesus knew but who he loved. 'He loved his own who were in the world' (13:1). And he adds, 'He loved them to the end'. This has two meanings and both of them are true: he loved them until the end of his life and 'he loved them in a way that surpassed all imaginable loving'.[4] He loves to the end, no matter that they run away when he most needs them. He loves them.

That is the rest of the gospel story: the death of Jesus makes known his love for his own and so God is known. (Remember John 3:16 again?) The verbs are in the past tense. He knew. He loved. Jesus' death is the hour of his leaving this sphere of everyday events and passing over to the Father. This is the ultimate act of love as he gives himself for the world.

Now in that room he teaches them of this love in a startling but memorable way. Love is shown in action. So with all that he knew and with all that love, what did Jesus do? He washes smelly feet. By this disconcerting gesture, 'Jesus embodies a new existence of loving, humble service in the world'.[5]

Chapter Nine

For Jesus there is no anxiety about his status or identity. He does not have to prove anything. In that awareness he begins the task. What are the tools of his trade as a Son sent from the Father? A towel and a basin.

Our tools define our trade. A computer? A lathe? Books? Our tools define our business and declare in part who we are. The tools of Jesus here are the tools of a lowly slave of that day. This is a lowly menial task — the washing of dirty, smelly, calloused, bleeding and bruised feet. This is not the job of a manager or a boss. This is the job for the lowest of the low. His tools are a towel and a basin.

Peter's agitated response and his dialogue with Jesus are instructive. He blurts out what possibly they all felt. This doesn't feel right! 'Not my feet!' Jesus' reply is to make clear that at the moment, Peter does not really understand what is happening. 'You do not know now, but later you will understand' (13:7). What would happen afterwards? Something is yet to happen when the disciples' ignorance will be transformed.

Still Peter opposes the idea of the washing of his feet. Jesus spells it out. This is something with a deeper meaning. 'Unless I serve you in this way, you cannot have any part with me.' 'Well', blustering Peter responds, 'give me the whole bath then!'

Peter has not understood, as readers of John do, that these conversations have a deeper meaning. Jesus does not give up on Peter but patiently explains that a cleansing touch from him, not a physical washing, is all that anyone needs. You are all clean (apart from Judas) because you follow me and love me.

What are we to make of all this? Peter is simultaneously humble enough to see the incongruity of Christ's action, and yet proud enough to want to dictate to his Master. He is 'fallible but redeemable' and so contrasts with Judas who chooses the devil and darkness.[6]

Even more, the foot washing anticipates all that was to come, and to come very soon. It is a parable of love in action. Just a few hours later Jesus was to be crucified. In the telling of the foot washing, John has an eye on the greatest sacrifice that is coming. Indeed, here is where we see that Jesus truly loved until the end: he cried, 'It is finished!' (19:30). The word for 'laid aside' his clothing

(13:4) is the same word in 10:15 where the Good Shepherd 'laid aside' his life for the sheep. His story is interpreting the cross for us. He is stripped down for service just as rough and insensitive soldiers will soon strip him naked.

As Richardson puts it, 'It foreshadows the cross itself: the voluntary humility of the Lord cleanses his loved ones and gives to them an example of selfless service which they must follow'.[7] Peter is told that there is no place in his company for those who have not been cleansed by his sacrificial death.

William Temple notes that every disciple must begin by allowing Christ to serve him or her. We too shrink from the idea that Christ would kneel before us. Peter is loyal and generous but it is only a false reverence and not faith that refuses to allow Christ to wash him. 'We need to learn that [our] first duty is to let Christ serve us.'[8] The church is always to receive first. Only after he gives us his grace can we serve.

This story is not about allowing Christ to wash someone else's feet. It is about allowing Jesus to put his hands on our feet. As someone has said, 'The act is shocking in its simplicity, its sensuality, its spirituality'. If we will not allow him to cleanse our feet, our story with him stops now. 'Only if I wash you can you have a share in me.' Will we allow Christ to serve us?

3. Jesus and our mission today (13:12–20)

The foot washing of the disciples, says C. K. Barrett, is 'at once exemplary, revelatory and salutary'.[9] It reveals Jesus' love. It is salutary in the sense that it represented a real act of cleansing which did not need to be repeated.

But it is also an example, as 13:12–20 makes clear. 'I have set you an example, that you also should do as I have done to you' (13:15). Jesus defines for us what our task is meant to be.

Barclay says the world is full of people who are standing on their dignity when they ought to be kneeling at the feet of their friends.[10]

Should we actually practise foot washing, as some churches do, at least occasionally?

Robert Herhold writes:

> It's probably just as well that foot washing never became a sacrament. Church property committees would not take kindly to pans of dirty water on the new carpet in the chancel. If theologians had gone to work on the question, we would still be embroiled in endless debate as to whether the feet should be immersed or sprinkled. Liturgists would argue whether the right foot or the left foot should be immersed first. Others would speculate on the symbolism of baptizing heads or feet. It's always easier to follow Jesus in our heads than it is to follow him with our feet on the Via Dolorosa.[11]

This is probably true though I have known foot washing as an occasional symbolic act to be rich with meaning and deeply moving for participants.

More deeply, we must recall that we have the same tools. A towel and a basin. Someone has suggested that a towel is not firm but manageable. It is flexible; it receives shape not from my hands but from the feet around which it is draped. The tool is shaped by the need of those being served; it does not come in a rigid shape.

So we are to follow his example and kneel before those in need. If you kneel before someone you become vulnerable, you are in an excellent position to have your face kicked in. So, again, Jesus is our example. He comes as a lowly servant, vulnerable and meeting our needs.

This perception of our mission might well transform our church life: to kneel before those in need, to take the towel shaped around the realities of others' needs and make ourselves vulnerable as we serve them. We are to forget about our pre-packaged towels and programmed basins, and serve others where they are with what they most need.

So this encounter with Jesus leads us to reach out to others, to follow his example, to do as he has done. Let the word of Jesus be our challenge and encouragement, 'Whoever receives one whom I send receives me; and whoever receives me receives him who sent me' (13:20).

Discussion questions

1. Read Section 1: (13:1–2).
    - What do you understand by 'he knew that his hour had come'?
    - Read Romans 7:15–20. Does this resonate with the statement, 'Evil is personal'?

2. Read section 2 (13:4–20).
    - For Jesus, is 'love' a noun or a verb, a concept or an action?
    - In what ways is washing the disciples' feet 'a parable of love in action'?

3. Read section 3 (13:12–20).
    - Why do we find it difficult to sing this opening of Richard Gillard's song:
      Brother, sister, let me serve you,
      let me be as Christ to you;
      pray that I may have the grace to
      let you be my servant too?
    - How can we best 'wash another's feet'?
    - What do you think is involved in having Jesus 'wash your feet'?

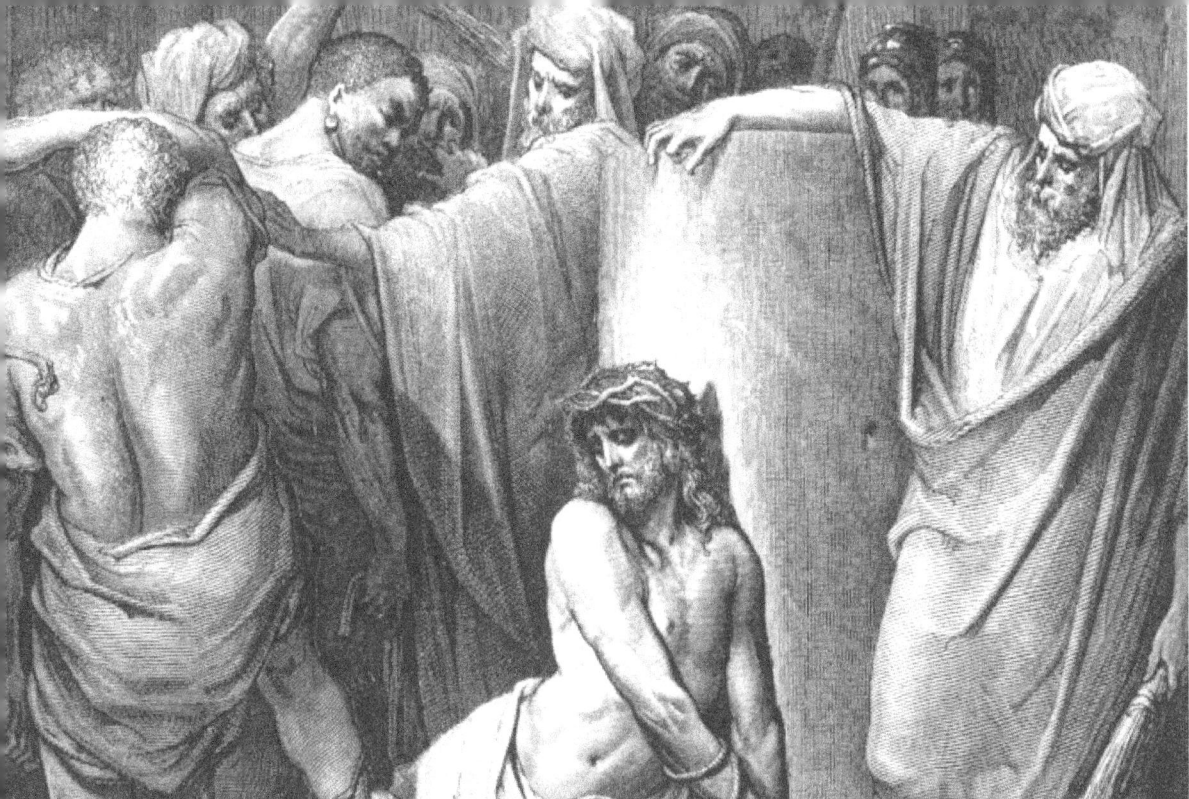

1800s, Jesus Is Scourged, Gustave Doré

Chapter Ten

'So you are a king?' —
Jesus and a governor
(John 18:28–40)

This encounter with Jesus in John's Gospel is significantly different from our earlier stories. Here we come to the climax of the gospel and the events of these last hours in the life of Jesus. These scenes have attracted readers across the centuries. Artists, poets, novelists, dramatists, scholars and theologians as well as countless humble believers have been fascinated by the drama and irony of this encounter — the representative of the mighty Roman emperor, urged on by a bloodthirsty group of religious fanatics, confronts a lowly teacher from the country region of Galilee in the remote province of Judea. One is a symbol of a violent military power, the other a preacher of peace and love. Their confrontation and conversation, especially as John tells it, are remarkable and surprising. For all readers, and especially for believers, here is a story of incredible sadness that never fails to involve and challenge us.

We are at once (18:28) introduced to the characters of Jesus, Pilate and the Jewish leaders and, as in all the encounters of this gospel, we are prompted to reflect on how something of ourselves may be seen in their actions, words and dilemmas.

The other gospels tell us about this trial of Jesus but in John we cannot miss that the theme of the kingship of Jesus dominates the narrative: it is stressed in the examination by Pilate (18:33, 37, 39), in the crude mockery of Jesus in the barbaric 'king-game' that cruel soldiers had devised to help pass the time (19:3), in the amazing shout by the Jews that their only king is the Roman emperor (19:14, 15) and finally in the words scratched onto a placard, 'Jesus of Nazareth, King of the Jews', an act designed to annoy the Jews but which became the proclamation that believers discerned to be the truth.

What kind of king is this strange man from Galilee? The question has echoed across the ages and comes directly to us in the quiet and comfort of our lives.

The story begins with a new day dawning (18:28), perhaps a hint that something new is happening in the history of the world. That morning was (probably) the day of the Passover when Jews recalled their delivery from Pharaoh and the Egyptians, when the blood of a lamb had been smeared over the doorposts of Israelite homes to ensure safety. And now 'the Lamb of God who is to take away the sins of the world', as readers of this gospel know (John 1:29), is presented for trial. These Jews offer up this sacred Lamb to an unjust heathen trial but remain outside the pagan *praetorium* (official residence of the governor) to avoid religious impurity: 'The strange creativity of religious ideology, prepared on the one hand, to make the Roman official complicit in its murderous intentions, yet, on the other, delicately observing ritual externals, is presented with piercing irony'.[1] What did they think God was like? How had the Passover come to such a lifeless end? How easily we can slip into a loss of perspective and proportion in our own living. How is it, for example, that male clergy can preach compassion but abuse children and women? We humans are strange creatures.

Chapter Ten

In John (18:29 – 19:16) the trial proceeds with a series of seven brief scenes that take place either inside or outside the *praetorium*. Inside stands Jesus, the truth and the light; outside are the Jews in the darkness, refusing to enter. Pilate moves between them, and the trial shows him making his reluctant choice.

1. Pilate and the Jews (18:29–32)

The central character is Pontius Pilate. A magnificent biography by Ann Wroe is called *Pilate: The Biography of an Invented Man*. The title is based on the fact that we really know very little about Pilate: one inscribed stone, a few coins, a few paragraphs in Josephus (a Romanised Jew who wrote 40 years after the governor was recalled from Judea), and a few pages in Philo, a Jew in Alexandria, as well as the New Testament documents. These suggest that Pilate was a thug, a cruel man and normally would be unlikely to show leniency to anyone brought before him.

Yet he has fascinated succeeding ages: a succession of apocryphal gospels, medieval writers and passion plays developed myths about his origins and later years. So the Pilate we think we know, says Wroe, is a mixture of dozens of invented men, each symbolic of something: 'The State facing the individual, the pagan world opposing the Christian one, scepticism versus truth, ourselves facing God… People ceaselessly project their own ideas and anxieties on him.'[2] Modern films have continued this process, perhaps reaching their nadir in the comic, lisping Pilate of Monty Python's (1979) *Life of Brian* ('Whom shall I cwucify? I shall cwucify Wobert!')[3]

Tony Blair suggested it was possible to view Pilate as the 'archetypal politician' and his dilemma, caught between what he thought was right and what was expedient, is 'a timeless parable of political life.'[4]

To find the real man in our story is a challenge but certain aspects of his character do emerge in this encounter. Passover was often a troubled time and most of the revolts that involved Jews took place about this season. That is why Pilate was in Jerusalem and not in his palace at Caesarea.

Caiaphas, that wily old High Priest of the temple, was a supreme political operator who had built a strong alliance with the occupying Romans and had determined that Jesus must be sacrificed if the Jewish leaders' power was to be maintained.

So, these two — and others of the Jewish leaders — all played their parts. Yet in John we also know that a divine plan was unfolding, the 'hour' when Jesus would be glorified, when he would be 'lifted up'. So when Pilate tried to send Jesus back to the Jews since their charges were vague and unsubstantiated, they insisted that they could not put anyone to death (although stoning for moral sins was, as we have seen, not beyond them). But as the gospel tells us (18:32), this by-play would ensure that what Jesus had said about his death would come true: he would be lifted up on a cross, as only the Romans could do (12:32–33).

As Pilate rolled out of bed that day to face some hours of troublesome business, he could not have known that this would be one of the most momentous days in human history and his own role would never be forgotten. Indeed, his very name would be remembered daily as countless people affirmed their creed and honoured the Christ who 'suffered under Pontius Pilate'. His inclusion in the Christian creeds, in the words of Archbishop Robert Runcie, 'binds the eternal realms to the stumbling, messy chronology of earthly time and place'. So our own little routines of daily demands can bring surprising possibilities of eternal significance.

2. Pilate the Governor and Jesus the King

Pilate goes back inside (18:33). Pilate and Jesus face each other on grotesquely uneven terms. How did this conversation take place? Did Pilate speak Greek, the language which Jesus probably knew too? Was there an interpreter? Is this a possible reason for misunderstandings? John is not interested in such questions and their dialogue is compelling. As Wroe says, 'However obtuse or thuggish Pilate is… there comes a moment when God, or the notion of goodness, disturbs him. He comes to a point where he can choose the higher or the lower path'.[5]

Dennis Potter imagines him taunting Jesus with his teaching that we should love our enemies. 'What about me?' he asks. 'Do you love me?' Jesus looks at him steadily and says, 'Yes, Pontius'.[6] Although this is an imaginary exchange, the sense of Jesus as the one in control is true to the gospels and who could doubt that

Potter has captured the strength of the one on trial.

Pilate is the one who asks about kingship. Jesus gives an enigmatic but gentle answer (18:34). Clearly this was what the Jews had said. Was it an appeal to Pilate's conscience? If so, the possibility is rejected with a snort. 'Am I a Jew?' 'Was he one of that tribe, bearded, atheist, fanatical, circumcised? All his Roman dignity burned in his face.'[7] 'Your people have brought you to me. What have you done to turn them against you?'

Jesus' answer only added to Pilate's confusion. 'My kingdom is not of this world. If my kingdom were from this world, my followers would be fighting to keep me from being handed over to the Jews. But as it is, my kingdom is not from here' (18:36). He does not speak about himself as king, but about his kingdom.

A kingdom not of this world? This was clear to gospel readers but surely was almost meaningless to Pilate! A realm without palaces, armies, violence? The last phrase is literally, 'my kingdom is not from here'. Pilate could have asked what is the theme of the gospel, where are you from? But he clutches at one idea, a seeming admission of being a king and scornfully asks, 'So, you are a king?'

What sort of king? Bruised face, blackened eyes, dirty robe and seemingly all alone. Again Jesus responds, 'You said it' (18:37). And he goes on to speak about truth; the truth that the gospel has taught us is found in this strange, seemingly powerless king. He offers Pilate a glimpse of a new reality but Pilate fails to listen to that voice.

Pilate's retort, 'What is truth?' has never ceased to echo and scholars have tried to interpret what he meant. He cannot step into Jesus' kingdom of truth and does he here brush it aside with a sceptic's remark? Is he just weary of the world and all its complexities? In any case, in Bacon's famous quip, 'jesting Pilate' would not stay for an answer and went outside again to the Jews. Deals have to be made.

3. Jesus the King most wonderful

The story unfolds in an agony of injustice and cruelty. Pilate declares that Jesus is innocent and offers them the choice: Barabbas or Jesus? The terrorist, the man of violence, is preferred to Jesus the man of peace. In order to assert his power,

Pilate orders Jesus to be flogged and the familiarity of that story should not stop us again realising the agony and cruelty of that scene. The mockery of rough soldiers, the grasping hands stripping his clothes and dressing him with the royal colour of purple, the bashing of that sensitive body, the mock coronation, with thorns pressed into that sacred head and the laughing shouts of 'Hail' which they normally gave only to their emperors and heroes. It was a great joke! King of the Jews! 'More than they deserve, these crazy people', they thought. 'He's a king for them!'

Pilate tries. Again, he goes out (19:4) and gives his verdict: not guilty. Then Pilate's famous introduction, 'Behold the Man!' What did he mean? *Ecce Homo* were words that thrilled Victorian-age writers and it became a sentimental note of adoration. Was it an appeal to their basic humanity? Just look at this poor fellow! Can you not see the blood, the wounds, the humiliation? But it was too late. The famous response was screeched out, 'Crucify!' Pilate tried again, 'You take him! He is innocent!'

Pilate was now terrified. Why? Romans didn't show fear. This is not fear of the mob, but a mounting sense of alarm. There is enough truth in Pilate to declare Jesus innocent, but political realities envelop him. He begs Jesus to tell him. 'Where are you from?' This is a question that is repeatedly found in this gospel. He doesn't mean 'Are you from Galilee?' because he knew that! He grasped at what Jesus had said before the whipping and the bashing.

Jesus is silent. The time for words has passed. The governor blusters about his power. Jesus then speaks and in effect says, 'Against me you have nothing — you are powerless and all that you have is from a God who is busy working his purposes out in this awful mess'.

This is indeed a strange king, 'a king most wonderful', as we like to sing. Pilate again goes out and we know what happened. You cannot reason with a mob. The crowd is unteachable. Why did this Roman hand over authority to the whim of a crowd who shouted out for Barabbas and the crucifixion of Jesus? They mockingly tell him what his job is — you will not be a friend of Caesar! The threat works its power over the Roman. Fear wins and injustice follows. The crowds and now the imperial power are puppets in the hands of political experts.

Chapter Ten

In a remarkable moment of ultimate betrayal, the descendants of Abraham, and David, and all the great people of faith and courage from their revered past cry out, "We have no king but the Emperor!" And all this at the Passover, on the anniversary of freedom from the pharaoh, the pharaoh is embraced'.[8]

Pilate went back inside, this time finally. Pilate had endured a difficult day and he was ready for his lunch.

What are we to say about Pilate? After Pilate's muddling actions, not even the symbolic washing of hands (as in Matthew 27:24) could change his fate. In some legends he later becomes a Christian but there is no historical evidence for that.

Ann Wroe concludes her portrait of Pilate in this moving way:

> He was the essence of evil or the essence of goodness: God's rejecter or God's embracer. These opposing legends had taken on lives of their own. Yet they had both sprung, however far back, from a civil servant's moment of uncertainty. There had been potential in Pilate at that moment for darkness or light far beyond the routine experience of a Roman prefect. Even he seemed to sense it. The tiny seed had lodged in his heart or his mind, suggesting infinite possibilities. He could take untravelled roads, open hidden doors, escape the bounds of earth and flesh, exceed himself. Or he could stay as he was: shrug, scratch his ear, write another memorandum.
>
> He stayed as he was. As most of us do.[9]

But none of us needs to stay that way. And the reason is found in that strange king. After his farce of a trial, Jesus the king then ascends his throne, a wooden cross. He is lifted up to die.

That torture and execution were bloody and meant to inflict excruciating agony. We have too readily sanitised the horror of it. As Lenny Bruce once quipped, 'If Jesus had been killed twenty years ago, Catholic school children would be wearing little electric chairs around their necks instead of crosses'.[10]

Yes, the worst that evil people could do happened to him. But as John insists, this was his hour of glory. God took this evil and made it the greatest good for all humanity. How has John told us? 'God so loved the world that he gave his only

Son, so that everyone who believes in him may not perish but may have eternal life' (3:16). All that terror, that anguish, that weakness, that death, all was a matter of obedience by this precious Son. Yes, he had come as the everlasting Word but his own had rejected him and now ordinary folk like you and me can hear the promise that all who do receive him, who do believe in his name, are given power to become children of God (1:12).

'So you are a King?' Pilate asked the question of the bound man before him. We ask the same question today.

As the answer is given to us through the pages of Scripture, will we shrug it off, cynical and jaundiced by our experiences in life? Or will we seek his truth in our lives? Will we shout with the crowds, cheering for some popular figure? Or will we bow before him?

We adore that loving Servant King. We follow him and crown him as king of our lives. But to follow such a king, to live in his kingdom that is not of this world, to hear his word of truth, is never easy.

This story of an encounter asks us to review our loyalties. *Who sits on the throne of my life?*

Let our prayer be:

> King of my life, I crown thee now
>
> Thine shall the glory be.

Chapter Ten

Discussion questions

1. Pilate and the Trial of Jesus (John 18:29 – 19:16).
   What are Pilate's actions in relation to Jesus in those 'seven brief scenes… either inside or outside the *praetorium*'?

2. Read section 1: (18:29–32).
   Is it true that, 'our own little routines of daily demands can bring surprising possibilities of eternal significance'? What difference does this make to our living as Christians?

3. Read section 2.
   - What evidence does John offer to illustrate the sense that Jesus was the one in control before Pilate?
   - What indications are there in this chapter that Pilate would have concluded, 'Deals have to be made'?

4. Read section 3.
   - In these events, what are some of the elements that make for such surpassing irony?
   - Read the quotation from Wroe beginning, 'He was the essence of evil'. Discuss the conclusion, 'He stayed as he was. As most of us do'. Is that true?
   - What do you know of the nature of the kingdom of 'that strange king'?

1601-1602, *The Incredulity of Saint Thomas*, Michelangelo Merisi da Caravaggio

Chapter Eleven

'What do you do when you're not sure?' — Jesus and a doubter
(John 20:19–31)

'What do you do when you're not sure?' This is the opening line in John Patrick Shanley's 2005 Pulitzer play, *Doubt*. The character Father John Flynn sets the stage for a story of suspicion and moral uncertainty with that question. His colleague, Sister Aloysius, is an old-school nun who suspects Father Flynn of improper conduct. We never know in the play whether he is guilty or not of what she suspects but doubt makes for powerful drama because doubt can be so destructive.

In this story we meet Thomas, a disciple who wasn't sure about Jesus' resurrection. We have been reading together stories of encounters between Jesus and various characters in John, mostly of different people on the way to faith: Mary at Cana, Nicodemus, the Samaritan woman, the woman taken in adultery, the blind man, Mary anointing Jesus, and one who turned away from any possibility of faith: Pontius Pilate. This gospel began with a series of faith journeys and here again in this chapter we find various ways in which disciples came to believe in the resurrected Jesus.

They did not find faith easily. Thomas had special difficulties, but Mary and the other disciples also came to faith in varied ways, reminding us that faith is not the same experience for us all: some find that faith is born and grows as quietly as a child sleeping on a mother's lap. For others, faith is a lifetime of questioning and wrestling with the claims of faith. Some cannot remember when they did not believe, others cannot remember anything else since their lives were shattered and reshaped by the decision of faith.[1] So none of these stories is normative for how we may come to faith, but all of them invite us into the circle of belief (20:30–31).

Our special focus is on Thomas, the disciple dubbed (probably unfairly) 'doubting Thomas' throughout history. He challenges us to explore the question of how we can really know the truth. That great philosopher of modern times Donald Rumsfeld notoriously posed the question as he commented on the Iraq war:

> As we know, there are known knowns. There are things we know we know. We also know there are known unknowns. That is to say we know there are some things we do not know. But there are also unknown unknowns, the ones we don't know we don't know.[2]

Of course, some doubt is inescapable in many aspects of life. In politics there is often doubt about the truth of what we are told. In law we can only ever hope for 'beyond reasonable doubt'. The scientific method is motivated by doubt: how can we be sure? Climate change is the latest challenge: some are 'believers' and others proudly proclaim their scepticism. Business, family life and marriage relationships can all be eroded by a lack of trust. What do you do when you're not sure?

There are three aspects of Thomas's journey of faith that can help us as we face our own doubts. As Witherington suggests, Thomas is to be seen as 'representative of more than just himself. He is a type.'[3] His pilgrimage shows how such a person can move to a robust and complete faith. Or as Raymond Brown puts it, this is why John has included this story: Thomas has become 'the personification of an attitude.'[4]

Thomas is a man with whom many of us most easily identify; is he the disciple for the twenty-first century? He is more of a realist than a doubter.[5] It wasn't easy for him. He had not been there on that special Sunday. That is not a criticism but a circumstance — he had not heard what Mary had to say, he had not seen Jesus, the Holy Spirit had not been breathed upon him. He had not been sent to bear witness to Jesus. Now he declares that he must touch in order to trust.

1. Doubt is not unbelief

There are a few references to Thomas in John and these suggest that he was a rather prosaic and practical man, a man of action rather than a deep thinker. (See 11:16; 14:5.) Now his friends are saying that Jesus is alive. They certainly seemed to be excited but he had to be sure. This was too important just to take their ecstatic claims at face value. Were his friends deluded? Had it been a case of wishful thinking? Was it what we would now knowingly call 'post-traumatic stress'? Had they drunk too much wine and then a kind of hysteria had set in?

After all, Thomas had been there on that fearful dark day and saw the wounds: the nails hammered into those gentle hands and his exposed side pierced with a cruel soldier's lance. He had been a part of the fulfilled prophecy, 'they will look on the one whom they have pierced' (19:37; Zech 12:10). He saw his beloved teacher and friend die on that miserable hill. With that death, all his hopes and dreams seemed to die too. Now they were saying Jesus was alive. How could he be sure?

So he laid down his faith condition: 'I want to see and touch those sacred wounds for myself. Then I will be sure, then I will be able to believe' (20:25). Thomas sets up his own criterion for belief. He must have his own encounter. He is not interested in some mystical ghost that may have popped in to scare the wits out of his friends (see Luke 24:37). He wants to know that it is his friend, the one who was crucified; no other will do! For all his bravery, he lives behind his own locked doors, shutting out whatever is outside the range of his imagination.

Some have judged Thomas harshly for this insistence: this is disbelief, this is demanding 'signs' — and Jesus had condemned those Jews who had pressed to see signs and wonders before they would believe. That clearly is a possible reading of the text.

But I do not think we should see Thomas in this way. After all, when Jesus came to the disciples a week later and Thomas was there, what happened? Did Jesus condemn him? Is not the point of the episode reached in 20:29: 'Have you believed because you have seen me? Blessed are those who have not seen and yet have come to believe'? In telling the story of Thomas, John is concerned with the great multitude, the community of disciples who cannot see Jesus or touch his side, but are yet called to faith. That is the nature of faith — it is not seeing, it is not having absolute physical evidence. Moreover, faith is always a gift or blessing: 'Blessed are those….'.

Frank Rees has a fine book, *Wrestling with Doubt*, in which he insists that doubt is ambiguous.[6] It can be negative, it can lead to unbelief and often does just that. But doubt does not have to separate us from the community of faith or from Jesus, and can also lead to faith. That is the message, and indeed, the hope of this Thomas story. Doubt, as such, is not unbelief. It does repeat our question, 'What do you do when you're not sure?'

2. Doubt is confronted by the Risen One

Jesus knew what Thomas had said. As Carson suggests, this shows that Jesus hears his disciples even when he is not physically present.[7] And what did Jesus say first to Thomas? 'Put your finger here and see my hands. Reach out your hand and put it in my side. Do not doubt, but believe' (20:27). Was this an accusation? A judgement? Was Jesus declaring, 'Thomas you are only a doubter?' He gives Thomas an invitation to touch him and so meet his human condition of faith. We are not told whether Thomas did touch Jesus or not; I suspect he did not.

What is more important is that Jesus treats Thomas as one of his people. He was with the disciples, a week after that first appearance. It is for Thomas now to take a further step in the process of faith. It is how God deals with us — he converses with us and invites a response. Thomas is asked not to move from disbelief (or an absence of faith) but from a form of faith which has not reached the full possibilities of peace and joy that the risen Jesus gives. Faith for Thomas is going with Jesus. It is an act of courage. Move from the air of doubt to the new atmosphere of faith!

That is why the climactic confession of faith in the whole Gospel of John comes from Thomas, 'My Lord and my God' (20:28). He knows!

Yet we must be clear. John is teaching us that although this is, at one level, how Thomas comes to faith, it is about the way in which he is changed by God's self-revelation. Jesus calls him to an ultimate point of self-surrender: 'The act of faith is only explicable by the act of the free self-disclosure of God'.[8]

Still, it is a deeply personal faith. As Schlatter observed, 'Through his single word "my" Thomas's knowledge remains not just knowledge but becomes faith'.[9] Or perhaps, we might say, 'This kind of knowledge is faith'. This is what you do when you're not sure! Faith is 'essentially relational and attitudinal'.[10]

3. Doubt is best faced within the community of faith

Thomas stayed with the disciples, questions and all. Thomas was not rejected because of his questioning. They were companions with him and helped him so that eventually he became the one who most powerfully expressed the faith that they had all been growing towards.

The church should be a community where there is an openness to those who have honest doubts and are seeking to know about the reality of faith. Thomas's question, 'Did this really happen?' is the one we still ask. It is 'our single most existential question'.[11] Thomas is every generation's seeker, one who hopes to know without any shadow of a doubt.

Dr Val Webb, an Australian theologian, in her moving book *In Defence of Doubt: An Invitation to Adventure*, recalls much of her personal journey.[12] She tells how the church of her youth suppressed all her questions and doubts. This had a negative impact on her life, leading to isolation, exclusion and repudiation. As

Chapter Eleven

Frank Rees comments, we all too often practise a form of 'theological abuse' that creates victims out of doubters.[13] An authoritative and dominating understanding of authority in the church can isolate true seekers.

No, the church is meant to be a place where honest doubt is welcomed and where faith is seen as a journey, and different people may be at different points along the way in that journey.

Do you recall how Matthew ends his gospel? Yes, we have the Great Commission in 28:19–20. But have you noticed what it says in verse 17? The 11 (so Thomas was there) went to Galilee to the mountain where Jesus had directed them. When they saw Jesus they worshipped him, 'but some doubted'. What, among the 11? This is not a reference to unbelief as such and some translate it as 'some hesitated'. Hesitation in action, but not in belief. Remember how Jesus was always telling the disciples (in Matthew) not to be fearful, but to have faith? The opposite of faith may in fact be fear.

They had reason to be afraid. But the call was to go beyond their 'little faith' to the next stage of faith. Jesus was with them and that is what made the difference. That is why they could fulfil the Great Commission, 'Lo! I am with you always'.

Tradition tells us that Thomas went as far as India preaching the gospel of the risen Jesus!

Once again, we are asked the question: Where am I in all of this? Am I willing to face my doubts and meet the risen Lord who alone can transform my life? Let us doubt our doubts. We may ask for faith. It is always a blessing, a gift (20:29; Ephesians 2:8). We cannot expect to see Jesus standing before us and inviting us to touch his wounds, but we can join that great community of faith who as Peter told a group of scattered Christians, 'although you have not seen him, you love him; and even though you do not see him now, you believe in him and rejoice with an indescribable and glorious joy' (1 Peter 1:8). As John told us early in the gospel, it is like being born into a new family (1:12).

I hope this story gives you help in answering an old question, 'What do you do when you're not sure?'

Discussion questions

1. As you have read these chapters, which of the encounters with Jesus on the way to faith have you identified with?
   - Explore the definition of faith (as given in the introduction) that faith is 'a mixture of mental conviction and existential commitment'.

2. Read section 1.
   - What is the logic that underlies the negative perception of him as 'Doubting Thomas'?
   - Explore the idea that doubt is ambiguous: it can lead to unbelief or it can lead to faith. How should we react to people who express doubts about Jesus?

3. Read section 2.
   - What is meant by the statement, 'the act of faith is only explicable by the act of the free self-disclosure of God'? Can you identify with Thomas in experiencing faith as 'essentially relational and attitudinal'?

4. Read section 3, 'Doubt is best faced within the community of faith'.
   - What differences do you see between the attitudes of atheism, agnosticism, disbelief, unbelief, little faith, faith and fear? Might they be stages on a spiritual journey?
   - For this to be so, in what ways would a community of faith need to act as Jesus did to deserve being called a true 'community'?

1400s, The Miraculous Draught of Fishes, Conrad Witz

Chapter Twelve

'But do you love me?' — Jesus and a guilty friend
(John 21:1–19)

Here we are at the end of John's Gospel. Actually, some scholars think we were there earlier because 20:30–31 sounds like an ending. After all the joy, excitement and commissioning of those resurrection appearances the gospel story seems to start again. Perhaps chapter 21 is a kind of epilogue, although all the oldest texts we have include this chapter — it has always been a part of John's Gospel as we have received it.

Haven't you sometimes wanted to add something to what you have said or written? I know that concluding a talk or a sermon can be a problem for inexperienced speakers — they hover like a helicopter but do not know where to land. But this is different. John had something important to tell us, even if it was added later.

After all, what do you do after Easter? Peter said, 'I'm going fishing'. Do you sometimes feel that when we celebrate Easter the Sundays afterwards are a bit flat? Christ is risen! Hallelujah! Meanwhile, back at the church, what do we do next?

This story is a guide to how we should live in the 'between times', after Christ has ascended and before his return. We know that the journey continues, we are still on the way to a deeper experience of God.

Peter is a key figure. The thrice-repeated question, 'Do you love me?' leads to his forgiveness and commissioning and these are central to our story along with the situation of the 'beloved disciple'. Is that why the chapter was added — to clarify their roles in the post-Easter church?

The stories about the appearances of the risen Jesus nearly always end up with Jesus commissioning someone. The presence of Jesus is linked with the sense of calling; if we read this story with faith and imagination we too should be prepared for the challenge and invitation to follow Jesus.

1. Peter and the disciples go fishing (21:1–14)

The scene for the last of our encounters with Jesus in this gospel is quickly set. We are alerted to the fact that this is a further appearance of the risen Jesus and we are back at Lake Tiberias or Galilee where seven of the disciples have gathered and where, as John told us (back in chapter 1), Jesus first called some of these men to follow him. Peter resolves to go fishing and his friends decide to come too.

Why did they go fishing? Fishing is an honourable trade, as it had been for Peter. But after all that they had seen it does seem a bit prosaic and speculations about their reasons have multiplied. Was it a turning away from their calling as disciples and a resumption of 'normal' living and working? Was it the result of a kind of aimless disorientation? Your guess is as good as anyone else's since we are not told, but I like the comment of Beasley-Murray, 'Even though Jesus be crucified and risen from the dead, the disciples must still *eat!*'[1] We are advised that after a long night's toil they had not caught one solitary fish. Even a non-fisherman like me can empathise with that.

Then follows a miracle. Jesus is on the beach in the dimness of a breaking dawn. He takes the initiative and asks if they have caught anything. As with some other appearances, they do not recognise him. He then directs them to cast their net out to the right side; they obey and instantly make a huge catch.

The beloved disciple is the first to realise what is happening and whispers to Peter, 'It is the Lord'. Peter then characteristically throws all caution to the wind, adjusts his scant clothing and leaps into the water. They bring the boat ashore and join Jesus and Peter on the shore where Jesus has a charcoal fire burning and is preparing a breakfast of fish and bread. He had been the host before the passion and now again he is the host at a meal they share.

John notes that none of the seven dared to ask him, 'Who are you?' because they 'knew it was the Lord' (21:12). That seems a strange comment. Burge explains, 'He is the same Jesus, but the events of Easter have also made him unspeakably different'.[2]

The fish caught that day numbered exactly 153 and ever since, people have been guessing what that number might symbolise — as many interpretations as there were fish, suggests one writer. Of course it just might be that was the actual number, remembered because it was so unusual. Fishermen love to tell tales about their experiences. A. M. Hunter suggests the number is no more symbolical than the hundred yards that Peter swam![3] The story is not an allegory but does have profound spiritual and moral lessons.

The net did not break and this is where we may justifiably find symbolism: disciples out fishing and not catching a thing. Follow the directions of Jesus and a marvellous catch ensues from which not one is lost. You don't have to be a great Bible scholar to interpret that as a promise for the following mission of the church as Peter and his successors become fishers of people. As Temple put it, 'The work which we do at the impulse of our own wills is futile'.[4] But with Jesus guiding us, our work is blessed.

Beside Lake Galilee is still a beautiful setting and I recall with gratitude a visit to the Holy Land many years ago when as a group we too had breakfast at the side of that lake, near the spot where tradition suggests this encounter occurred.

But it must have been a difficult moment for Peter. A *charcoal* fire? Remember how Peter had stood at night warming himself at another charcoal fire and when challenged, denied any knowledge of Jesus, not just once but three times. Then he heard the crowing of the rooster. Now here he was with Jesus. With his scarred hands, Jesus handed the bread and the fish to Peter and his friends, a scene that inevitably made them and makes us think of that last meal in the upper room when Jesus broke bread and spoke of giving his body for them. Was it not in the breaking of the bread that those disciples on the road to Emmaus recognised Jesus as their companion (Luke 24)?

How would Peter feel? What would Jesus say? Without this last chapter we could not have known, and that is perhaps why it was written.

2. The question from Jesus we all must face: do you love me?

After breakfast we may imagine Jesus strolling along the lakeside with Peter, and the others walking behind at a respectful distance. Everyone knew this was an intimate moment for these two, master and disciple, to resolve the tension between them.

Back at the beginning of their journey together Jesus had told 'Simon son of John' that he would be called Peter or 'rock-man' (1:42). Some rock he had turned out to be! Peter must have thought that so often in those few hours and days. It is worth noting that Jesus here again calls him by that old name 'Simon son of John'.

And what does Jesus say? He doesn't mock Peter but gently asks him, 'Do you love me?'

That is a question that has been asked so often across the ages in so many different situations, but most commonly, I guess, between people in the most intimate of relationships such as a man and his wife. Some find it easier to talk about love than others.

Older ones among us will recall that fabulous musical *Fiddler on the Roof*, set in a small Jewish peasant community in old Russia. The central character Tevye asks his wife Golda, 'Do you love me?' Startled, she responds, 'Do I what? Do I love you?' Confused she sings, 'Your daughters are getting married, you're upset, is it indigestion? Go inside and lie down'.

He again asks, 'Do you love me?' 'You're a fool… I'm your wife… For 25 years I've washed your clothes, cleaned your house, cooked your meals, given you children, milked the cow — I've lived with him, fought with him — after 25 years why talk about love right now?' 'Then you love me?' 'I suppose I do.' 'And I suppose I love you too.' 'After 25 years it's nice to know.'

Many of us, older males particularly I fear, have the 'of course I love you' attitude. You don't have to be a marriage counsellor to know that relationships don't survive on such attitudes.

But this exchange by Galilee is different. For some it might seem decidedly odd to imagine a spiritual leader asking his follower if he loves him. For many modern people it is perhaps even harder to talk about love in a religious relationship. It seems sentimental and unreal. But if you think about it, the Bible is absolutely full to overflowing with this kind of challenge. God loves his people and asks for their love. Jesus was asked, 'What is the first and greatest commandment?' His answer was, 'Love the Lord your God with all your heart, soul, strength, and mind' (Matthew 22:37).

No, the most basic assertion we can make about God, as this gospel has stressed, is that *God loves us*. As we are, undeserving and needy. Without reserve. So much, as John puts it, that he gave his only Son for us. Again and again, talking with his disciples, Jesus had patiently taught them about love. Back there in that upper room on that fateful night he had talked about love: 'I have loved you, just as my Father has loved me'. Love each other. The greatest way to show love for friends is to die for them. Love each other, over and over again. Indeed, in 1 John which comes from the same tradition as this gospel, the ultimate assertion is made, 'God is love' (I John 4:8).

Do you remember that story about Mary and that extravagant gift of love as she poured the perfume over the feet of Jesus? Jesus welcomed her love and rejected the grumbles of Judas who would soon betray Jesus with the symbol of love, a kiss.

But it was in that same room on that same night that Peter had blurted out, 'I will follow you anywhere, I would die for you!' (13:37). Jesus then told him that before a rooster crows he would say three times that he didn't even know him. So on that beach Jesus now asks his would-be follower, 'But do you really love me?'

What exactly did Jesus ask? Do you love me 'more than these'? More than what? Several possibilities have been suggested. Do you love me more than these nets and fishing and your old life? Do you love me more than you love these fellows here? Do you love me more than these fellows love me?

Whatever the precise nuance of the question the common reality is that true love is always exclusive. Peter's reply is instant, 'Yes, Lord! You know that I love you' (21:15). More than fishing! More than these friends! More deeply than I can imagine anyone else loving you! The raw emotion in Peter's answer is transparent. But again and yet a third time the same question is asked. Peter's anguish is intense — 'Lord, you know everything, you know I love you'.

No cock crowed. However, not only Peter, but all readers ever since cannot miss the meaning. Three times a denial, and now three times a question about love. Jesus' response each time was: 'Then show your love by caring for my sheep'. He had taught them to think of him as the great shepherd who would even die for his flock. 'Now, Peter, I want you to be a shepherd, a pastor to my flock, to my church, to my lost and bleeding people. Look after them no matter what it costs you.'

In the Greek text different words for 'love' and for the 'flock' (lambs, sheep) and the task (feed, tend) are used and some try to find hidden depths in the words written, but there is one question and one task to which Peter is called. Years later, when he wrote to church leaders in what we call First Peter, he passed on the task to a new generation of church leaders:

> Tend the flock of God that is in your charge, exercising the oversight, not under compulsion but willingly, as God would have you do it — not for sordid gain but eagerly. Do not lord it over those in your charge, but be examples to the flock. (1 Peter 5:2–4)

For Peter and for us the charge is simple but costly: care is a basic component of a Christian lifestyle.

That is why we still read this story. We see Peter being given another chance, to claim the grace of another day. We too are there, as it were, by that lake. We know what it is to have failed, to have denied Jesus and to have fled from the smallest challenge to our faith. Can we hear the question, 'Do you love me?' More than anyone and anything? Can we receive the grace and gift of another day? And he wants to charge us with the costly care of all those he loves so deeply still.

It isn't enough to say, 'For all these years I have done this and done that for you'. That is not his question. Do you recall in Revelation (also linked by tradition with John) that the church at Ephesus was praised for all that it had done, but the risen Christ made that sad criticism, 'You don't have as much love as you used to. Think about where you have fallen from, and then turn back and do as you did at first' (Revelation 2:4–5)?

A disciple being asked about his love for Jesus? A church not loving Jesus as once they did? Uncomfortable and sentimental it may sound to a cynical and weary world, but for all true believers the question comes full of both challenge and hope, 'Do you love me more than... what?' (fill in the blank).

So Peter did become a rock. Jesus warned him, *When you are old ...* (21:18). Others will lead you and take you where you don't want to go. Sadly, that is true in so many ways for many of us when we grow old. No more energy, no longer able to lead, no longer able to choose our own way, strapped in by a belt in a car seat and taken off to another doctor.

But have not God's people been told that it is in weakness that we find the true depths of God's grace and strength? Old age is the time for new and different experiences of grace. Frederick Buechner states, 'I have always trusted God with my life. The change is that now I begin at last to trust God with my death'.

Of course for Peter it meant something else. It meant he would die a martyr, as he almost certainly did away in distant Rome in the time of that cruel emperor Nero. But Peter could not have understood all that, then, there by the lake. But unburdened of the destructive memories of failure and called again to service, Peter was a new man who was able to face whatever the future held.

Peter still had a long way to go. As he walked along (I imagine them arm in arm), he looked back at those trudging behind and almost tripped over himself as he saw the beloved disciple and could not help himself. 'What about him?' Jesus must have been frustrated as he told Peter, 'That is not your business — you just follow me!' (21:20–22). Your discipleship is not to be confused with another's. Both were serving the same Lord and both were called to follow him in a way that was true to their special calling.

The final word to Peter is the same word still spoken to us, 'Follow me!' I remember seeing a cartoon in a book of prayers where a blindfolded disciple says, 'It's all very well saying, "Follow me" but where on earth are we going?' Well we might ask.

How could Peter know where Jesus was taking him? Jesus ascended into heaven and did not occasionally pop up in a room or by the lake. How could Peter follow if he could not see Jesus? He had been told. In that same upper room. Jesus would send his Spirit and he would guide them; that's how they would know where Jesus wanted them to go. Wanting Peter, for example, to open the doors of the church to all who sought Jesus, not just those of a Jewish background. Leading Peter to go to Rome — that great metropolis so far from the quietness of Galilee and there face the ultimate test of his love and loyalty.

What about us? Follow me. Don't look back and worry about how well or badly anyone else is doing. Follow Christ. T.W. Manson once wrote, 'The living Christ has two hands, one to point the way, and the other held out to help us along'.[5]

Have we heard and answered the question, 'But do you love me?'

I hear Jesus asking me: *Ken, son of Bert, do you love me more than these?* Can you hear your name, too? Will you join me in a quiet but sincere answer: 'Yes, Lord, you know I do'? Will we stay to hear Jesus say, 'Follow me! Care for others!'?

This is the end of John. But encounters with Jesus have never ceased. As T. R. Glover wrote, 'The Gospels are not four, but ten thousand times ten thousand and thousands of thousands, and the last word of every one of them is, "Lo I am with you always, even unto the end of the world"'.

Discussion questions

1. Read section 1, Peter and the disciples go fishing (21:1–14).
   - As we read this story, identify with the disciples. What characteristics of Jesus might they have recalled, and what other factors might have stimulated their memories?
   - What emotions might those recollections have evoked?

2. Read section 2, the question from Jesus we all must face: do you love me?
   - When one person says to another, 'I love you', what is implied by that assertion?
   - When Jesus asks Peter, 'Do you love me?', it is suggested that 'this exchange by Galilee is different'. In what ways, would you think?
   - What depths underlie Jesus' persistence in questioning Peter three times about his love?
   - What are the elements in our story of Jesus and Peter by the lake that can lead our study towards its concluding challenge, 'Follow me! Care for others!'

3. Read John 20:30, 31. How has John helped us believe that Jesus is the Son of God?

CONCLUSION

A recent successful film called *The Way* (2010) depicts the journey undertaken by a small group of individuals on the historic *Camino de Santiago* (the Way of St James), a Catholic pilgrimage route to the Cathedral of Santiaga de Compostela in Galicia, Spain. The central figure is Tom Avery, an American ophthalmologist who travels to France following the death of Daniel, his adult son, killed in the Pyrenees during a storm while walking the pilgrimage route.

Tom initially travels simply to retrieve his son's body. But in grief and in honour of his son, Tom decides to walk the ancient trail where his son had died. As the French police officer tells Tom, 'The Way is a very personal journey'.

As he walks in his lonely isolation he meets others also on the way. They are travelling for their own reasons which also prove to be painful. Gradually an unlikely quartet travel together and meet diverse strangers who are also on the pilgrimage route. Finally they reach the Cathedral and each makes a personal response in that beautiful sanctuary. For Tom his peace comes when, finally at the ocean's edge, he commits the last remnants of his son's ashes to the water. The concluding scenes show Tom, now a different man, transformed by his experience of travel on the way and enjoying a more meaningful life.

This film reminds us that we too are invited to walk the way of discovery. Tom does not discover Jesus in any obvious way in the film, but he is changed, and the hope of peace that Jesus offers is at the heart of the ancient pilgrimage tradition.

The image of life being a journey is of course a wellworn motif. The journeys of the ancient people of Israel in the Old Testament shape much of the New Testament's understanding of the church: they are a pilgrim people (see 1 Peter 2:9). The famous theologian Augustine expounded this idea in his classic work, *The City of God*. Numerous works of devotion have explored this way of interpreting Christian life, none more loved than John Bunyan's *Pilgrim's Progress*. More recent writers have explored the ideas of 'an outward journey' and 'an inner journey' to describe individual disciplines and attitudes as well as discovering new ways of service.

In this simple study of encounters between diverse people and Jesus in the Gospel of John, we too have been invited to explore the possibility of making our journey of discovery. It is a very personal journey. Our readings have prompted us to see how different individuals, in quite diverse ways, have been changed by meeting Jesus.

We have also learned that sharing with others in community helps us in our quest, as the story of 'doubting' Thomas shows. We may all be at different points on the way to faith but to walk together is a fundamental aid in discovering who Jesus is and the deepest purpose of our lives. John certainly wrote so that we might believe that Jesus is the Christ, the Saviour of the world, but his gospel repeatedly shows that we are called to walk this way in the company of other disciples.

We have stressed that faith is a mixture of mental convictions and personal (existential) commitment to Jesus. Perhaps we can identify with the rough hard-working fishermen, or with the learned theologian, or with a woman whose past immorality had seemingly determined her identity forever. All found that Jesus met their deepest needs.

Perhaps we have been on the way for a long time. Doubts, personal failures and guilt, a fear of commitment or some other issue has prevented us moving further along the way to genuine and complete faith. But as we read Scripture and especially John, as we engage with contemporary witnesses to his love, as we welcome the gentle inner promptings of the Spirit, we too may discover the risen Jesus.

John admitted that the world could not contain all the books that could be written about Jesus (21:25). In so far as these modest reflections on the encounters with Jesus point to the witness, transforming power and authority of Scripture, we dare to share the same specific goal as the gospel writer confessed, 'These are written so that you may come to believe that Jesus is the Messiah, the Son of God, and that through believing you may have life in his name' (20:31).

READING GUIDE

The New Revised Standard Version (1989) has been used unless otherwise indicated.

The following commentaries on John have been found most useful.

Barclay, W. *The Gospel of John* (Daily Study Bible, 2 vols; Edinburgh: Saint Andrew Press, 1955).

Barrett, C.K. *The Gospel According to St. John* (2nd edn, London: S.P.C.K., 1978).

Beasley-Murray, G.R. *John* (Word Biblical Commentary, 36; Waco: Word Books, 1987).

Brown, R.E. *The Gospel According to John* (2 vols, Anchor Bible 29, 29a; New York: Doubleday, 1966–70).

Bruce, F.F. *The Gospel of John* (Basingstoke: Pickering &Inglis, 1983).

Bruner, F.D. *The Gospel of John. A Commentary* (Grand Rapids: Eerdmans, 2012).

Carson, D.A. *The Gospel according to John* (Grand Rapids: Eerdmans, 1991).

Craddock, F.B. *John* (Knox Preaching Guides; Atlanta: John Knox Press, 1982).

Keener, C.S. *The Gospel of John. A Commentary* (2 vols, Peabody, Mass.: Hendrickson, 2003).

Kelly A.J. and F. J. Moloney, *Experiencing God in the Gospel of John* (Paulist Press: New York, 2003).

McHugh, J.F. (ed. G. N. Stanton) *John 1 – 4: A Critical and Exegetical Commentary* (International Critical Commentary; London: T & T Clark, 2009).

Moloney, F.J. *The Gospel of John* (Sacra Pagina, 4; Collegeville, Minn.: Liturgical Press, 1998).

Morris, L. *The Gospel According to John* (New International Commentary; Grand Rapids: Eerdmans, 1995).

Temple, W. *Readings in St John's Gospel* (London: Macmillan, 1961[1939–40]).

Westcott, B.F. *The Gospel according to Saint John* (London: John Murray, 1908).

Witherington III, B. *John's Wisdom. A Commentary on the Fourth Gospel* (Louisville,Ky: Westminster John Knox Press, 1995).

Endnotes

Preface

1   J. Claypool, *The Preaching Event* (Waco, Tx: Word, 1980), p. 28.

2   As quoted by F.D. Bruner, *The Gospel of John: A Commentary* (Grand Rapids: Eerdmans, 2012), p. 255.

3   E. Brunner, *The Divine–Human Encounter* (Trans. A.W. Loos; London: SCM, 1944).

4   A. L. Griffith, *The Crucial Encounter: The Personal Ministry of Jesus* (London: Hodder and Stoughton, 1965).

Introduction

1   T. Silvers in The Age, Jim Stynes supplement, 21 March 2012, p. 2.

2   R. Dawkins, *The God Delusion* (London: Black Swan, 2007), pp. 112–117.

3   As quoted by F. D. Rees, *Wrestling with Doubt: Theological Reflections on the Journey of Faith* (Collegeville, Minn.: The Liturgical Press, 2001), p. 186.

4   B. Witherington III, *John's Wisdom: A Commentary on the Fourth Gospel* (Louisville: Westminster John Knox, 1995), p. 69.

5   A. J. Kelly and F. J. Moloney, *Experiencing God in the Gospel of John* (Paulist Press: New York, 2003), p. 3.

Chapter One

1   F. B. Craddock, *John* (Atlanta: John Knox Press, 1982), p. 9.

2   W. Temple, *Readings in St John's Gospel* (London: Macmillan, 1961 [1939]), p. 27.

3   J. F. McHugh (ed. G. N. Stanton), *John 1 – 4: A Critical and Exegetical Commentary* (International Critical Commentary; London: T & T Clark, 2009), p. 150.

4   Bruner, *The Gospel of John*, p. 102.

5   Temple, *Readings in St John's Gospel*, p. 28.

6   'The summons' by John Bell, No. 363 in Baptist Praise and Worship (Oxford: OUP, 1991).

Chapter Two

1. Daily Telegraph (UK) 7 October 2008.
2. Bruner, *The Gospel of John*, p. 127.
3. Bruner, *The Gospel of John*, p. 132.
4. J. F. McHugh (ed. G. N. Stanton), *John 1 – 4*, p. 181.
5. Witherington, *John's Wisdom*, p. 79.
6. Witherington, *John's Wisdom*, p. 82.
7. K. Coffey, 'The Cana Couple Reminisce', *Theology Today* 48 (1992), p. 459.

Chapter Three

1. <www.metrolyrics.com/born-again-lyrics-third-day.html> accessed 23 March 2013.
2. As quoted by Witherington, *John's Wisdom*, p. 92.
3. Witherington, *John's Wisdom*, p. 104.
4. C. K. Barrett, *The Gospel according to St. John* (2nd edn, London: S.P.C.K., 1978), p. 172.
5. As quoted by Bruner, *The Gospel of John*, p.172.
6. F. Buechner, *Peculiar Treasures: A Biblical Who's Who* (New York: Harper & Row, 1979), p. 122.
7. Bruner, *The Gospel of John*, p.174.
8. F. F. Bruce, *The Gospel of John* (Basingstoke: Pickering & Inglis, 1983), p. 90.
9. J. F. McHugh (ed. G. N. Stanton), *John 1 – 4*, p. 240.

Chapter Four

1. D. A. Carson, *The Gospel according to John* (Grand Rapids: Eerdmans, 1991), p. 21.
2. Claypool, *The Preaching Event*, p. 127.
3. F. B. Craddock, 'The Witness at the Well (John 4:5–42)', *Christian Century*, 7 March 1990, p. 243.
4. F. B. Craddock, *John*, p. 38.

Chapter Five

1 Carson, *The Gospel according to John*, p. 334.

2 Bruner, *The Gospel of John*, p. 506.

3 As quoted by F. J. Moloney, *The Gospel of John* (Sacra Pagina, 4; Collegeville, Minn.: Liturgical Press, 1998), p. 262.

4 See <wcc-coe.org/wcc/assembly/chall.html> accessed 23 March 2013.

Chapter Six

1 'Open this book that we may see your word' by Christopher Ellis, No. 103 in *Baptist Praise and Worship* (Oxford: OUP, 1991).

2 W. Styron, *Darkness Visible: A Memoir of Madness* (New York: Random House, 1990).

3 C. S. Keener, *The Gospel of John. A Commentary* (2 vols, Peabody, Mass.: Hendrickson, 2003), p. 775.

4 Source unknown.

5 As quoted by Bruner, *The Gospel of John*, p. 577.

Chapter Seven

1 J. Howard, *Lazarus Rising* (Sydney: Harper Collins, 2010).

2 E. H. Peterson, *The Message: The Bible in Contemporary Language* (Colorado Springs: NavPress, 2002).

3 L. Newbigin, *The Light Has Come. An Exposition of the Fourth Gospel* (Grand Rapids: Eerdmans, 1982), p. 142.

4 As quoted by Bruner, *The Gospel of John*, p. 659.

5 G. Campbell Morgan, *The Four Gospels* (London: Oliphants, 1956), p. 197.

6 Kelly and Moloney, *Experiencing God in the Gospel of John*, p. 249.

7 As cited by W. Barclay, *The Daily Study Bible: The Gospel of John* (Edinburgh: Saint Andrew Press, vol. 2, 1956), p. 119.

Chapter Eight

1. In his poem, 'Lichtenberg' (1901).
2. E. Moltmann-Wendel, *The Women around Jesus* (New York: Crossroad, 1982), pp. 51–58.
3. Moltmann-Wendel, *The Women around Jesus*, p. 58.
4. W. Temple, *Readings in St John's Gospel*, p. 184.
5. R.H. Lightfoot, *St. John's Gospel. A Commentary* (Oxford: OUP, 1960 [1956]), p. 236.
6. Moloney, *The Gospel of John*, p. 358.
7. See the article by Lawrence Money, '"Curly" giving hope to thousands', The Age 29 April 2010.

Chapter Nine

1. Craddock, *John*, p. 98.
2. 'Meekness and Majesty' by Graham Kendrick, No. 58 in *Baptist Praise and Worship* (Oxford: OUP, 1991).
3. As cited by Bruner, *The Gospel of John*, p. 748.
4. Moloney, *The Gospel of John*, pp. 373–74.
5. Kelly and Moloney, *Experiencing God in the Gospel of John*, p. 277.
6. Witherington, *God's Wisdom*, p. 235.
7. As cited by L. Morris, *The Gospel according to John* (Grand Rapids: Eerdmans, 1971), p. 612.
8. Temple, *Readings in St John's Gospel*, p. 205.
9. Barrett, *The Gospel according to St. John*, p. 367.
10. W. Barclay, *The Gospel of John*, vol 2, p. 162.
11. R. H. Herhold, 'Foot Washing and Last Things (John 13: 1–20)', *Christian Century*, 9 March 1983, p. 205.

Chapter Ten

1. Kelly and Moloney, *Experiencing God in the Gospel of John*, p. 356.
2. A. Wroe, *Pilate: The Biography of an Invented Man* (London: Vintage, 2000), p. xiv.
3. Wroe, *Pilate*, p. 34.
4. Wroe, *Pilate*, p. 208.

5   Wroe, *Pilate*, p. 225.

6   Wroe, *Pilate*, p. 226.

7   Wroe, *Pilate*, p. 226.

8   Craddock, *John*, p. 134.

9   Wroe, *Pilate*, p. 365.

10 Dawkins, *The God Delusion*, p. 285.

Chapter Eleven

1   Craddock, *John*, p. 142.

2   The statement was made by Rumsfeld, the United States Secretary for Defense on February 12, 2002 at a press briefing where he addressed the absence of evidence linking the government of Iraq with the supply of weapons of mass destruction to terrorist groups.

3   Witherington, *John's Wisdom*, p. 339.

4   R. Brown, *The Gospel according to John* (Anchor Bible, 2 vols, Garden City, New York: Doubleday, 1966–1970), p. 1031.

5   Witherington, *John's Wisdom*, pp. 346f.

6   F.D. Rees, *Wrestling with Doubt: Theological Reflections on the Journey of Faith* (Collegeville, Minn.: Liturgical Press, 2001), p. 198.

7   Carson, *The Gospel according to John*, p. 657.

8   Kelly and Moloney, *Experiencing God in the Gospel of John*, p. 384.

9   As quoted by Bruner, *The Gospel of John,* p. 1183.

10 Rees, *Wrestling with Doubt*, p. 186.

11 Bruner, *The Gospel of John*, p. 1185.

12 V. Webb, *In Defence of Doubt: An Invitation to Adventure* (St Louis, Mo: Chalice Press, 1995).

13 Rees, *Wrestling with Doubt*, p. 127.

Chapter Twelve

1 G. R. Beasley-Murray, *John* (Word Biblical Commentary, 36; Waco: Word Books, 1987), p. 399.

2 G. M. Burge, *John* (NIV Application commentary; Grand Rapids: Zondervan, 2000), p. 584.

3 A. M. Hunter, *The Gospel according to John* (Cambridge Bible Commentary; Cambridge: Cambridge University Press 1965), pp. 194–95.

4 Temple, *Readings in St John's Gospel*, p. 379.

5 T. W. Manson, *Ethics and the Gospel* (London: SCM, 1960), p. 68.